Sarah Flower, a leading nutritionist and author of many cookery books, is passionate about healthy eating and is a keen advocate of the sugar-free and low-carb way of eating. She has trained with the Real Meal Revolution, who specialise in LCHF and Banting, and she is also a Banting coach in the UK.

Sarah writes for a number of publications, including the *Daily Mail*, *Top Santé Magazine* and *Healthista*. She appears regularly on BBC Radio Devon and BBC Radio 4's Woman's Hour.

Also by Sarah Flower

The Sugar-Free Family Cookbook

The Busy Mum's Plan-ahead Cookbook

Eat Well, Spend Less

The Healthy Lifestyle Diet Cookbook

The Healthy Halogen Cookbook

The Healthy Slow Cooker Cookbook

Perfect Baking with Your Halogen Oven

Halogen Cooking for Two

The Everyday Halogen Family Cookbook

The Everyday Halogen Oven Cookbook

Slow Cook Fast Food

Low-Carb Slow Cooker

Quick, Delicious and Sugar-Free
Slow Cooker Recipes for All the Family

Sarah Flower

ROBINSON

ROBINSON
First published in Great Britain in
2017 by Robinson

1 3 5 7 9 10 8 6 4 2

A CIP catalogue record for this book
is available from the British Library.

ISBN: 978-1-47213-957-3

Typeset in Enigma and Source
Designed by Andrew Barron
Printed and bound at Mohn Media
in Germany

Papers used by Robinson are from
well-managed forests and other
responsible sources.

MIX
Paper from
responsible sources
FSC® C104740

Robinson
An imprint of
Little, Brown Book Group
Carmelite House
50 Victoria Embankment
London EC4Y 0DZ

An Hachette UK Company
www.hachette.co.uk

www.littlebrown.co.uk

_____

How To Books are published by
Robinson, an imprint of Little, Brown
Book Group. We welcome proposals
from authors who have first-hand
experience of their subjects.
Please set out the aims of your book,
its target market and its suggested
contents in an email to
Nikki.Read@howtobooks.co.uk

_____

The recommendations given in this
book are solely intended as education
and should not be taken as medical
advice.

Contents

Preface

I am a passionate advocate of the low-carb lifestyle, having myself followed a low-carb, high-fat (LCHF) diet (also known as the Banting diet), which also includes an avoidance of sugar, for a couple of years now. I have also placed several of my clients on this regime with amazing results. It is an honest way of eating – avoiding processed foods, and opting instead to eat real food, high in natural fats, and moderate in protein and low-complex carbohydrates. This book is a natural follow-on from my *Sugar-Free Family Cookbook*, which also adheres to low-carb principles. I adore using my slow cooker, so combining the positive benefits of slow cooking with low carb is a perfect fit for me.

I want to encourage you to eat lots more good fats – such as oily fish, good oils, nuts and seeds – all of which will have calorie-counting experts jumping up and down with frustration. We need oil in our diets – it is crucial for good health inside and out, so those who advocate a strict low-fat diet will not only suffer from more ill health, but also start to go wrinkly quicker!

One of the other drawbacks of low-fat diets is that when people concentrate so much on things being low in fat, they forget to look at what else is going on in their diet. Low-fat diets can often be high in carbohydrates (and I'm talking the bad carbs – think white flour, sugar, white pasta and so on). They are often low in fibre and lack essential fatty acids.

I recommend using more natural sugar substitutes such as xylitol, erythritol blends like Sukrin or Natvia, or stevia – all of which are explained in Chapter 2 (see pages 10–12). There is a very strong link between obesity and our consumption of sugary foods – hence my strictness when it comes to using sugar. It is in everything we eat, and when we have high levels of sugar, it converts to glucose and can raise our blood sugar levels. To stabilise this and remove dangerous glucose from our bloodstream, our body produces insulin. However, the glucose isn't broken down and excreted as we may hope, but is converted to fat. Sadly, not only does our body convert excess glucose into fat, but it can also inhibit us from breaking down that fat. I won't get too technical, but please trust me on this; if you only take one thing from this book it is to reduce or ideally eliminate sugar. I know xylitol, erythritol and stevia are more expensive to buy than sugar, but their health benefits are huge. As you progress on your low-carb journey, you will crave less and less sugar.

Do take the time to look at the informative chapters at the beginning of the book – they are there to help and support you on your journey towards better health, and also include information on how to use your slow cooker.

I always welcome emails from readers and any feedback on how you get on with my books. Visit my website at www.sarahflower.co.uk., where you will also find links to my Facebook groups and pages. I also update new recipes and ideas on my blog, so keep a lookout for them, and you can follow me on Twitter – MsSarahFlower. If you have enjoyed this book, I hope you will recommend it to others.

Good luck and good health.

Sarah Flower

Conversion charts

Weight

METRIC	IMPERIAL
25g	1oz
50g	2oz
75g	3oz
100g	4oz
150g	5oz
175g	6oz
200g	7oz
225g	8oz
250g	9oz
300g	10oz
350g	12oz
400g	14oz
450g	1lb

Oven temperatures

CELSIUS	FAHRENHEIT
110ºC	225ºF
120ºC	250ºF
140ºC	275ºF
150ºC	300ºF
160ºC	325ºF
180ºC	350ºF
190ºC	375ºF
200ºC	400ºF
220ºC	425ºF
230ºC	450ºF
240ºC	475ºF

Liquids

METRIC	IMPERIAL	US CUP
5ml	1 tsp	1 tsp
15ml	1 tbsp	1 tbsp
50ml	2fl oz	3 tbsp
60ml	2½fl oz	¼ cup
75ml	3fl oz	⅓ cup
100ml	4fl oz	scant ½ cup
125ml	4½ oz	½ cup
150ml	5fl oz	⅔ cup
200ml	7fl oz	scant 1 cup
250ml	9fl oz	1 cup
300ml	½ pint	1¼ cups
350ml	12fl oz	1⅓ cups
400ml	¾ pint	1¾ cups
500ml	17fl oz	2 cups
600ml	1 pt	2½ cups

Measurements

METRIC	IMPERIAL
5cm	2in
10cm	4in
13cm	5in
15cm	6in
18cm	7in
20cm	8in
25cm	10in
30cm	12in

1

How to use your slow cooker

Slow cookers gained popularity in the 1970s, but the principle of slow cooking goes back hundreds of years – think of the large stock pots seen dangling from ranges. Slow cookers were seen to revolutionise the kitchen, since they could create wholesome meals ready for your return after a busy day. They were incredibly popular, but sadly were relegated to kitchen cupboards as we moved into the Thatcher years of 'loadsamoney', when our need to live a frugal life ceased to have relevance. Cheaper cuts of meats stopped being popular, so there seemed to be no real reason to keep a slow cooker in our kitchens. The microwave oven and processed food became the housewife's choice for a busy home, and the poor slow cooker ceased to inspire. Thankfully, we are now seeing a revival of these clever machines as we realise that they can not only save us time, but are also superior nutritionally.

You can buy slow cookers from as little as £15, and there is an increasing demand for multi-cookers, of which I am a huge fan. When purchasing a slow cooker or multi-cooker, it is important to consider how it is going to be used. Think about the size of the machine. Some look quite big, but the actual size of the stock pot may not be as big as you need. If you are cooking for a large family or like to plan ahead and freeze food, you may be better off spending more money and investing in a larger machine. Go to an electrical store where you can actually view the machines – even if you don't buy one from the store, seeing a selection will give you an idea of the machines on sale and what your requirements are.

Multi-cookers

I am a massive fan of the slow cooker and thought I knew all there is to know about these machines. That was until I discovered the multi-cooker. Initially I thought it was a bit of a gimmick – stating that it can steam, slow cook, roast, sauté and bake – but it has won me over. I have reviewed several of these machines, but the Crock-Pot Multi-Cooker is the one I favour and has now taken pride of place on my kitchen worktop.

Some slow cookers have a sauté option, which allows you to sauté on five different temperature settings, though I've found this option a bit hit and miss. However, the multi-cooker really is an all-in-one cooking experience. The slow-cooker function allows you to choose high, low or warm settings. Once the cooking time has been reached, the slow cooker automatically switches to warm mode – perfect if you are late home for dinner. The roasting rack can be used on either a low or high setting, depending on the size of the joint you are cooking. When cooking a small joint of beef, for example, I seal it first with the sauté function, then add some vegetables to the base, before popping in the beef joint on top and switching the cooker to roast for forty-five minutes. The joint cooks perfectly, and the vegetables and juices at the base make a delicious stock. I allow the beef to rest, wash out the crock-pot bowl, add some water to the base and steam the vegetables in seven minutes. So easy.

To sauté or not to sauté

Recipes often tell you to initially sauté onions or brown meat. I have tried both including this step and omitting it, and to be honest I really did not notice much difference in flavour, though the colour of the ingredients is more appealing if you do brown them, and browning also helps to seal meat. If you are cooking a whole chicken, for example, it will not brown when cooked without sealing, so may look a little less appetising to serve. Sautéing chicken additionally prevents it from flaking into a dish. Coating meat with a low-carb, grain-free flour can also help if you want a thicker sauce – a slow cooker does not lose that much liquid, and you may find that you need to thicken the liquid in your dishes until you get used to the way your machine works. All multi-cookers offer a sauté option, and you may find that your slow cooker has a sauté facility; others come with hob-proof dishes, allowing you to transfer from one source to the other. You will need to refer to the manufacturer's instructions for more information about your machine. Each recipe details both techniques, allowing you to choose which one you prefer.

Cooking techniques

All slow cookers come with full manufacturer's instructions, recipe suggestions and even a useful helpline if you get stuck. I strongly advise that you read the instructions before using your machine. Here are some reminders:

◆ Some cookers need to be preheated, which can take up to 15 minutes; others heat up fast so you may not need to do this (refer to the manufacturer's recommendations).

◆ As a general rule of thumb, an hour in a conventional oven equates to 2–3 hours on high in a slow cooker, or six hours on low heat. Some slow cookers have an auto setting – this basically means that the cooker heats up quickly on high, and on reaching the required temperature, reverts to low for the remainder of the cooking. This helps food, especially meat, reach a safe temperature quickly. Some machines have a warm setting, which is useful when food in the cooker has reached its maximum cooking time and you just want to keep it warm. Really, however, the low setting is enough and food can cook for ten hours without starting to spoil.

◆ You may need to adjust the liquid content of a dish, depending on your personal taste, but bear in mind that you do need liquid in order to cook the food. All food must be submerged in the liquid before cooking. Potatoes especially may bob around on top and go black, so push them into the liquid. The manufacturer's guidelines should detail the minimum and maximum fill levels for your machine. Liquids do not evaporate as much in a slow cooker as they do when using other cooking methods, so you may need to thicken soups or casseroles. Adding more water or stock is simple, and can be done at any stage.

◆ The key point to remember about slow cooking is that once you begin cooking, you shouldn't keep removing the cooker lid. Doing so reduces the temperature, so that the cooker then needs to get back up to the required temperature. The outer edge of the lid forms a seal – sometimes the cooker contents may spit or bubble at this point, but this is quite normal. Only remove the lid when absolutely necessary – ideally just at the end of the cooking period, or if necessary in the last thirty minutes of cooking to add key ingredients. If you are the sort of person who likes to keep an eye on things, opt for a slow cooker with a glass lid (though this is not foolproof as these cookers do get steamed up).

◆ Always defrost any frozen ingredients (especially meat) thoroughly before placing them in a slow cooker. Though the machine is designed to cook safely at low temperatures, if it does not maintain the required heat it could increase the risk of food poisoning caused by the spread of bacteria. Frozen foods such as peas, sweetcorn, prawns and other quick-cook vegetables should only be added in the last thirty minutes of the cooking time.

◆ When adding liquids such as stock or water, it is best to use warm liquids (not boiling) rather than cold ones, in order to maintain the temperature.

◆ Pasta should only be added in the last thirty minutes of the cooking time as it goes very soggy and breaks up if it is cooked for longer.

◆ Fresh herbs can be used, but their intense flavours tend to be lost during long cooking times. If I am using fresh herbs, I add them in the last thirty minutes of the cooking time.

2

The low-carb store cupboard

This is a rough guide to what you need when you embark on a low-carb lifestyle based really on what I use. I personally try to use everyday foods so this list is quite basic. Remember you are not stocking up on lots of processed foods but making your own, even including condiments.

Natural sweeteners

Natural sweeteners should not be used as an excuse to eat loads and loads of sweet foods. They are a tool to help you in the transition phase to reduce your sugar cravings. The further down the road of sugar-free eating you go, the less you will crave sweet foods. You will also find that you can dramatically reduce the quantity of natural sweeteners in your recipes as your palate changes.

Xylitol

I use the Total Sweet brand of this. The name xylitol may sound slightly odd, but the word is derived from the Greek word for wood, *xyl*, as in xylophone, because the natural sugar alternative was first discovered in birch wood. Xylitol has now been found in a host of other plants and their fruits, such as sweetcorn and plums, but is still largely extracted from birch and beech woods in Europe today.

Xylitol looks and tastes just like normal granulated sugar, but it has a host of benefits. It has 40 per cent fewer calories than normal sugar, and less than 50 per cent of the available carbohydrates (those that are utilised by your body), but it *does* contain carbohydrates and therefore stimulates an insulin response, so is not suitable for everyone.

Xylitol can have a laxative effect in some people, particularly if eaten to excess. The laxative effect is caused because xylitol attracts water to it. This effect is different from one person to the next, and can change as your body gets use to xylitol. The lower your body weight the less xylitol it takes to cause the effect, so children can be affected more than adults. As a general rule, daily consumption should be limited to 5–10g per 10kg of body weight (adults and children alike).

You also need to keep xylitol, and any food made with it, well clear of dogs. As is the case with grapes and chocolates, dogs metabolise xylitol quite differently from humans and it can be very dangerous for them, even in small amounts. Don't be tempted to give your dog anything with xylitol in it, no matter how small. It could prove fatal for it.

Erythritol blends

I use Sukrin products, but you can also use the Natvia brand. You can buy icing sugar in both these ranges. Just like xylitol, this is another sugar alcohol known as a poll, found in grapes and pears. Use this as a direct replacement for sugar in recipes, but be aware that stevia is often added to these blends as erythritol on its own is not very sweet, so you may detect a slight aftertaste.

I really like Sukrin products, especially Sukrin Gold (a brown sugar alternative, see also below). You can buy Sukrin online or from good health food stores. Unlike other sugar-free, low-calorie substitutes such as xylitol, erythritol contains zero calories. Erythritol does not affect blood sugar or insulin levels during or after consumption, making it safe for diabetics and for those following a LCHF diet. It is a little more expensive than stevia, but personally I prefer it as I don't like the aftertaste you experience with Stevia, or some of the side effects of xylitol. You can find more information regarding Sukrin at www.sukrin.co.uk. Natvia is a new brand from Australia, and again very good. It is available in supermarkets.

Sukrin Gold

This is a great alternative to brown sugar that I use quite a lot to create a deeper sweet flavour.

Stevia

Stevia is a wild plant from subtropical forests in north-east Paraguay. Its leaves contain glycosides, the sweetening power of which is 250–400 times their equivalent in sugar. Stevia contains no calories and no carbohydrates. It does not raise blood sugar or stimulate an insulin response, so for many people it is the preferred choice.

Stevia is very sweet and the cheapest of all three sweeteners discussed here, but it does have a strange aftertaste that is hard to control. I have found that liquid stevia has less of an aftertaste, but it is really trial and error and depends on the brand you use. I have also found that some people are more sensitive to the aftertaste than others. Plus, you need very tiny amounts, so it's a bit of a juggling act to start with.

It is very hard to gauge how much stevia to use in recipes, as it is very much down to personal taste, the product and your sensitivity to the aftertaste. If you are new to this you may prefer to use xylitol or erythritol. If you are a fan of stevia, you can still follow my recipes, but add stevia to suit your own personal taste and requirements.

Store cupboard essentials

Nuts I use a lot of nuts – mostly almonds, pecan nuts, walnuts, hazelnuts, macadamia and Brazil nuts. I often blend fresh nuts to make nut butters and nut flours. I store unused nut flours in the freezer to prevent them from going rancid. Nuts are great for making your own granola and nut bars. You can also make spicy nuts and use them as a healthy replacement for crisps.

Cake recipes often call for almond flour. This is quite expensive, and you can use ground almonds instead. They are a little coarser in texture, but work just as well – I use them all the time.

Coconut I keep shredded coconut as well as desiccated coconut. I use shredded coconut in my granola and nut bars.

Coconut flour I don't use a lot of this (rather using ground almonds), but it is good to have in your store cupboard. It does absorb up to ten times its volume in liquid, so you may need to add extra liquid when you are using this flour. A good 'all-purpose' flour is three parts almond flour to one part coconut flour. Don't forget to use baking powder when making cakes.

Coconut oil This is absolutely essential as it is used in many recipes.

Chia seeds These little seeds are packed with goodness. They are great to use as a thickener, and make wonderful porridge and creamy desserts.

Whey powder I have not used whey powder in the recipes in this book, but I do use it to make a grain-free bread, find it useful in some grain-free cake recipes, and occasionally add it to smoothies. I buy organic, grass-fed whey powder.

Seasonings I use a lot of seasonings and make my own blends. It is best, if you can, to buy these in bulk as it will save money. I store the seasonings in small jars.

Cocoa/cacao Whether you prefer cocoa or cacao is a matter of personal preference. I prefer cacao as it is purer than cocoa, but some people find it too bitter. Look for sugar-free cocoa. If you can't get this, you may have to opt for cocoa and add a little more natural sweetener if you find it too bitter.

Dark chocolate You can buy 95 per cent dark chocolate that is excellent (Lindt brand). Also look out for dark chocolate chips, but do check the cocoa content – the ones in supermarkets only contain about 50 per cent cocoa. Go to a health food shop or look online for better options.

Gelatine I use gelatine powder by Great Lakes as I like the grass-fed, natural variety, but you can use sheets if you prefer.

Seeds I have a range of seeds in containers in my cupboard. Flax, sesame, pumpkin and sunflower seeds are the ones I use every day. I often sauté some seeds in coconut oil and add them to my salads to make a nice crunch and add nutrients. I also use seeds in my home-made bread and crackers, and top my yoghurts with them.

Apple cider vinegar I like to drink this every day as it has some amazing health benefits. I also add it to the pot when making bone stock, as it helps to draw out the nutrients. You can use it in place of white wine vinegar in salad dressings.

Xanthium gum You can employ this powder as a thickener if you don't use grains, instead of cornflour. Simply sprinkle on your dish and stir well. It's also sold as Xanthan gum.

Yeast extract I use this in my cooking as it can add a good flavour. Check that your brand is sugar free.

Tinned tomatoes You can always whip up a tasty dish if you have some tinned tomatoes. I always buy the best quality I can, as I find the taste far nicer than that of cheaper brands.

Sun-dried tomatoes in oil I love the flavour of sun-dried tomatoes, but check the labels as some brands contain lots of sugar. I always have a jar of them to add to food or turn into a paste.

Fridge

Vegetables and salads My fridge always has lots of salads and vegetables in it, including avocados – a must have! Don't let your avocados go off – you can freeze them. Frozen avocado is great to use in smoothies, guacamole and chocolate pudding.

Milk I use full-fat milk in my cooking and only keep semi-skimmed milk for visitors, for their tea or coffee, as I've found that most people prefer it. I drink mine black so can't comment on that one.

Cream I buy extra-thick cream to use for puddings. I also have double cream for making sauces and to add to dishes. Cream is essential for making your own ice-cream.

Yoghurt I only buy full-fat Greek yoghurt, and add my own berries and chopped nuts to it.

Eggs These are absolutely essential. I probably get through a least twenty-four eggs a week.

Butter Another essential. I do not use any margarine or spreads.

Cheese I always have full-fat cream cheese in my fridge as I use it for puddings, pizzas and even cakes, finding it to be a great binder. It is good as a creamy sauce. I keep a variety of cheeses, including extra-mature Cheddar, brie, halloumi, Stilton and feta.

Mayonnaise There is always a jar of home-made mayonnaise in my fridge, as I love to eat salads. I don't make up bottles of salad dressing. I tend to just make a small amount when needed, or drizzle salads with extra virgin olive oil or almond oil.

Extra virgin olive oil This is kept in a cool, dark cupboard, as heat, light and oxygen can destroy the nutrients and turn it rancid.

Berries For me, these are a must-have, though I only use a small handful at a time. I like raspberries and fresh blueberries the most. I find frozen blueberries have a very peculiar taste.

Bacon I don't eat loads of bacon, but it is always good to have it in the fridge. I like to bake it until it is very crispy, before chopping it into small pieces to add to a salad. I also use it in my main meals and, obviously, for breakfast. I buy good-quality bacon that is not packed with water. If possible, buy bacon from your local butcher – it does not cost much more than bacon bought at a supermarket, but is far superior in quality.

Meat and fish I buy free-range organic chicken. I use beef mince, but only if it's organic from the supermarket, or from local sources recommended by my butcher. I eat steaks with salads and also like to roast a gammon joint, using the cold meat in savoury snacks and omelettes. I tend not to buy sausages as they are full of grains, but there are now some good-quality sausages available in supermarkets containing more than 95 per cent meat (ask your butcher for recommendations). I buy fresh fish, but also keep some tuna steaks and salmon fillets in the freezer.

Carbonated sparkling water It's controversial, I know, as some people believe it stops you from absorbing nutrients. For me, it is a refreshing drink to have occasionally with slices of lemon and lime, and it can be good if you are withdrawing from a fizzy drink habit.

Freezer

I try to keep a range of home-made ready meals in my freezer for when I am busy and haven't got time to put something together. Always remember to label and date anything that goes in the freezer, or it may end up being in there for months longer than it should be!

Frozen berries I tend to opt for frozen raspberries because, as already mentioned, I find that frozen blueberries have a weird taste. I use these in a variety of recipes for things like ice-cream, desserts and even jelly berry bears.

Meat and fish Though I never buy frozen meat, I do have chicken, lardons, mince and steak in my freezer – this is often because I don't get around to eating it in time so pop it in the freezer. I also have salmon fillets and tuna steaks in the freezer.

Vegetables I keep frozen peas in my freezer. I process fresh cauliflower until it resembles rice in texture, then pop it into small bags and place them in the freezer, as I find I don't use a whole cauliflower at once. Cauliflower processed in this way can be used to make cauliflower rice (see page 195) or mash. Broccoli can be prepared in the same way.

Bones I buy a large bag of bones (about 4kg) from my butcher for around £2 a bag. This lasts me months. I slow cook, then store the bone broth in the freezer in small freezer bag portions. I also put some in a silicon ice-cube tray to pop out when I need to add a touch of stock to a dish.

3

Low-carb soups

Soups are bursting with nutrients. They are great for providing extra vegetables for your family to eat. They are also economical and easy to cook, and can be used as a snack or nutritious meal, as they are very filling. Best of all, your favourite recipes won't need much adapting when following a low-carb, sugar-free diet. The main thing to be aware of is your stock. Be careful with any shop-bought soups as they can be full of sugar, salts and other nasties. If you or your child has a packed lunch, why not invest in a small flask and fill it with your home-made soup – perfect to fill up and warm the body, especially during the winter months. Most soups can be frozen, so fill your freezer with individual portions ready for lunches.

Soup-making advice

Stock

Stock cubes can be quite overpowering and also high in salt and sugar. Ideally use home-made stock or even just water and fresh herbs, allowing the natural flavours to rule. At the time of writing, the only stock cubes I could find that were free from sugar were by a company called Kallo. They offer powders and cubes – not all are sugar free so you have to read the ingredients. I like the beef bouillon powder (though beef bouillon cubes contain sugar). You can also buy Marigold Swiss Vegetable Bouillon or Vecon concentrated vegetable stock. Most of these products are available from health food shops, but do check the ingredients list before buying. Try to make your own stock as it will be packed with nutrients, particularly if you use animal bones (see page 193 for bone stock recipe). You can freeze any stock you make, so cook it in batches. Where any of the recipes in this book include stock and you don't want to make your own, you can instead add a teaspoon of yeast extract with warm water or Bovril, which is sugar free (though cubes are not); again, check the ingredients. Marmite is sugar free but some other brands contain sugar. I do, however, recommend using bone stock because of its many health benefits.

Puréeing soups

Some people like chunky soups, while others like smooth ones. It is a purely personal taste. When puréeing a soup, I use an electric hand blender (some call it a stick blender). It is simple to use and saves on washing up and messy transfer to a liquidiser (make sure the end of the blender is fully submerged in the soup, or you will end up with it everywhere). For a really fine soup, you can filter the ingredients through a sieve.

Chunky soups

Some chunky soups may benefit from a thicker stock or sauce. To achieve this, simply remove about a quarter of the soup and purée it, then return the purée to the soup. If you want to make your own stock, recipes for bone and chicken stocks are included in Chapter 9 (see pages 193–4).

Liquid – thick or thin

You may need to adjust the liquid content of a soup depending on your personal taste. When cooking in a slow cooker, less liquid evaporates than when using other cooking methods, so you may need to thicken soups – to do this, add 1–2 teaspoons xanthium gum and stir well. Alternatively, you can make a thickener using a little coconut flour and water, mixed together until combined. If you don't mind employing grains, use cornflour with water. Place the thickener in the slow cooker, ensuring that it is evenly distributed. Turn the temperature to high and cook for 15–30 minutes until thick – alternatively, you can remove some of the chunky soup and purée it. Adding more water or stock is simple and can be done at any stage.

Pulses and beans

Adding pulses and beans to a dish is a cheap method of bulking out a meal. They also contribute essential nutrients to a dish and can keep you fuller for longer. Pulses and beans are, however, quite high in carbohydrates and for some, especially those following a LCHF diet, they are not permitted, so my recipes do not include them.

Creams

Creams, milk, Greek yoghurt and crème fraîche can sometimes separate when cooked in a slow cooker for long periods, so it's best to add them just before serving.

This is a lovely soup for autumn, when squash is readily available. You do not have to remove the skin – it cooks well and adds a nice flavour. I like the chilli yoghurt, but if making the dish for children you might want to omit the chilli. If you are dairy free, swap the dairy yoghurt for plain coconut yoghurt or coconut cream.

Butternut Squash Soup with Spiced Yoghurt

SERVES 4

Nutritional information per serving
129 kcal
3.9g fat
15g net carbohydrates
3.5g fibre
7g protein

1 red onion, diced
1–2 cloves of garlic, crushed
1 tsp coriander seeds, crushed
1 butternut squash (about 400g), deseeded and diced
400ml warm water, or vegetable or bone stock
1 tsp ground coriander
Seasoning to taste
200g Greek yoghurt
1 chilli, finely chopped
1 tsp hot paprika
Seasoning to taste

1 Preheat your slow cooker following the manufacturer's instructions.

2 Chop all the vegetables and add to the slow cooker. Cover with the warm stock and coriander, and season to taste.

3 Place on auto or high and cook for 6–8 hours.

When ready, taste to check the seasoning before liquidising the ingredients (I use my electric hand blender rather than transferring the ingredients to a liquidiser – this saves washing up!).

4 In a separate bowl, mix together the yoghurt, chilli and paprika.

5 To serve, place the soup in serving bowls and add a swirl or dollop of yoghurt in the centre of each.

This is one of my favourite soup recipes and it is the perfect choice if you need to fill yourself up with healthy fat when you are following a low-carb diet.

Broccoli and Stilton Soup

SERVES 5

Nutritional information per serving

211 kcal
11.5g fat
8.6g net carbohydrates
6.9g fibre
14.2g protein

1 red onion, finely chopped
1 stick of celery, finely chopped
750g broccoli, roughly chopped
450ml vegetable, chicken or bone stock
150g Stilton or other blue cheese
Seasoning to taste

1 Preheat your slow cooker or multi-cooker following the manufacturer's instructions.

2 Chop all the vegetables and place in the slow cooker.

3 Cover with the warm stock and cook on low for 6–7 hours.

4 Half an hour before serving, add the Stilton and stir well until it has melted. When ready to liquidise, use a stick blender to blend until smooth.

5 Season to taste before serving.

Forget those awful processed cuppa soups. This is the real thing – perfect to pop into a flask for your working lunch. This recipe includes chillies, which not only taste delicious but also help speed up your metabolism. If you don't fancy the heat, just omit the chillies – or avoid adding the seeds as these can make the soup much hotter.

Tomato and Chilli Soup

SERVES 4

Nutritional information per serving
101 kcal
0.9g fat
16.3g net carbohydrates
5.3g fibre
4g protein

1 red onion, finely chopped
2 cloves of garlic, crushed
1–2 chillies, depending on personal
   preference
800g fresh tomatoes, peeled and
   finely chopped, or use 2 x 400g tins
   of chopped tomatoes if you prefer
50g sun-dried tomatoes
1 stick of celery, finely chopped
350–400ml warm water, or vegetable
   or bone stock
1 heaped tsp paprika
Black pepper to taste

1 Preheat your slow cooker or multi-cooker following the manufacturer's instructions.

2 Make sure you cut the vegetables into roughly equal sized pieces so that they cook as evenly as possible. Add them to the cooker.

3 Cook on low for 6–8 hours.

4 When ready, liquidise the ingredients to a purée, adding more liquid if required.

5 Season to taste before serving.

6 Serve with a drizzle of chilli oil for an extra kick.

Did you know? *Tomatoes are rich in lycopene. According to a World Cancer Research Fund and American Institute for Cancer Research report, lycopene can reduce the risk of prostate cancer. Lycopene from tomatoes is more available and better absorbed by our body when the tomatoes are cooked, crushed or eaten with a little fat, such as olive, coconut or flax oil.*

This recipe uses bone stock. Sounds unappetising? Bone broth is really good for you and packed full of nutrients. If you don't fancy making your own, you can order it online and from some butchers.

Vegetable Soup

SERVES 6

**Nutritional information
per serving**
90 kcal
1.7g fat
11.7g net carbohydrates
3.5g fibre
4.7g protein

1 large red or white onion, finely
   chopped
2–3 cloves of garlic, finely chopped
1 red pepper, diced
2 sticks of celery, diced
1 carrot or ¼ butternut squash, diced
1 large courgette, diced
50g green beans, each cut into
   3 pieces
600ml bone stock
1 bay leaf
1 tsp paprika
Salt and pepper to taste
Parmesan cheese, grated, to flavour
   (optional)

1 Preheat your slow cooker or multi-cooker following the manufacturer's instructions.

2 Add all the vegetables, warm stock, paprika and bay leaf. Season well.

3 Cook on high for 6–8 hours.

4 Serve with a sprinkle of grated Parmesan cheese for added flavour.

I love this soup. It has a nice, creamy texture and is not too cheesy. My son loves it, too, though I have to keep the Stilton a secret – if he saw me put it in he wouldn't eat it! The blue cheese is quite salty so you need not add salt to the recipe.

Celery and Stilton Soup

SERVES 4

Nutritional information per serving
338 kcal
31.5g fat
5.1g net carbohydrates
1.9g fibre
7.4g protein

1 onion, finely chopped
25g butter
450g celery, finely diced
500–600ml hot vegetable or
   bone stock
150g Stilton cheese, crumbled
200ml double cream
Seasoning to taste, if required

1 If your slow cooker needs to be preheated, turn it on 15 minutes before using. Refer to the manufacturer's instructions for more information on your specific model temperatures.

2 Put all the ingredients in the cooker, apart from the cream and Stilton cheese. Make sure the stock is hot when adding it, as this will keep the temperature.

3 Cook on low for 6–7 hours, or if you want a faster meal turn to high for 3–4 hours.

4 Twenty minutes before serving, add the crumbled Stilton cheese and double cream. Allow the cheese to melt before liquidising gently. Season to taste if required.

5 Serve immediately, or remove and leave to one side until needed. The soup freezes well, or keeps in an airtight container in the fridge for 2–3 days.

Nettles are rich in iron and calcium, and really high in vitamin A. Made as a tea, they can help with urinary infections (the nettles act as a diuretic), and they have been shown to help protect against kidney stones. If you are dairy free, swap the double cream for coconut cream.

Nettle Soup

SERVES 4

Nutritional information per serving
373 kcal
28.9g fat
17.1g net carbohydrates
5.4g protein

1 large red onion, diced
1 clove of garlic, roughly chopped
2 sticks of celery, diced
500g young organic nettles (wear gloves if picking them yourself)
450ml hot vegetable or bone stock
200ml double cream
Black pepper and olive oil to taste

1 Wash and chop the nettles thoroughly (you may want to wear gloves for this). They will start to wilt if you run them under hot water, making it easier to pop them into the slow cooker later.

2 If your slow cooker needs to be preheated, turn it on 15 minutes before using. Refer to the manufacturer's instructions for more information on your specific model temperatures.

3 Put all the ingredients in the cooker, apart from the cream. Make sure the stock is hot when adding, as this will keep the temperature.

4 Set the slow cooker to cook on low for 5–6 hours.

5 Use an electric hand blender to purée the ingredients. Add the cream and stir well. Season to taste before serving. The soup benefits from a good dash of black pepper and sea salt, and a drizzle of olive oil.

I love tomato soup – if you like a bit of a kick, add some chilli flakes. For a creamy soup, stir in a couple of tablespoons of cream, crème fraîche or coconut cream before serving.

Tomato and Basil Soup

**Nutritional information
per serving**
92 kcal
0.8g fat
15.2g net carbohydrates
4.6g fibre
3.6g protein

1 red onion, diced
1–2 cloves of garlic, crushed
1 stick of celery, diced
750g tomatoes, diced (remove the
  skins if you like)
50g sun-dried tomatoes in oil,
  drained
1 tbsp tomato purée
2 tsp paprika
1 tsp dried basil
450ml vegetable or bone stock
Small handful of fresh basil, chopped

1 If your slow cooker needs to be preheated, turn it on 15 minutes before using. Refer to the manufacturer's instructions for more information on your specific model temperatures.

2 Put all the ingredients in the slow cooker, apart from the basil leaves. Make sure the stock is hot when adding it as this will keep the temperature.

3 Cook on low for 6–8 hours, or if you want a faster meal cook on high for 4–5 hours.

4 Twenty minutes before serving, add the fresh basil leaves.

5 Whizz with a hand blender before serving.

6 If you want a creamier soup you can stir in some cream, crème fraîche or coconut cream, or use it to form a swirl when serving.

This is a really nice soup, which is quick and easy to make. If you are following a diet, you may want to avoid this as it has a relatively high carb content due to the peas. If you are dairy free, you can swap the crème fraîche for coconut cream.

Creamy Pea Soup

SERVES 5

**Nutritional information
per serving**
268 kcal
17.4g fat
17.2g net carbohydrates
6.6g fibre
7.3g protein

1 red onion, finely chopped
2 sticks of celery, finely chopped
500g frozen or fresh peas
550ml vegetable or bone stock
Black pepper
Small handful of fresh mint or thyme
    leaves, finely chopped
200ml full-fat crème fraîche or double
    cream
Olive oil, to serve

1 If your slow cooker needs to be preheated, turn it on 15 minutes before using. Refer to the manufacturer's instructions for more information on your specific model temperatures.

2 Put all the ingredients in the cooker, apart from the mint leaves, and crème fraîche or cream. Make sure the stock is hot when adding it as this will keep the temperature.

3 Cook on low for 4–6 hours, or if you want a faster meal cook on high for 3–4 hours.

4 In the last 20 minutes, add the mint leaves and stir well.

5 Just before serving, take out a few peas to use as a garnish and whizz the remainder of the soup with your hand blender before stirring in the crème fraîche or cream. Taste, and add more black pepper if needed.

6 Serve immediately. Garnish with some mint or thyme leaves and the reserved peas, plus a drizzle of olive oil.

This is a lovely warming soup, perfect as a winter warmer. You can buy Harissa paste or seasoning, but ensure that it is free from sugar. The soup should be chunky, so make sure you chop everything evenly when you prepare the ingredients.

Chicken, Cumin and Harissa Soup

SERVES 5

**Nutritional information
per serving**
152 kcal
2.8g fat
6.5g net carbohydrates
1.7g fibre
24.3g protein

1 red onion, finely chopped
2–3 cloves of garlic, finely chopped
½ red pepper, finely chopped
1 tsp ground cumin
1 tsp paprika
2–3 tsp Harissa paste
400g tin of chopped tomatoes
400g chicken fillets, diced (thigh gives the best flavour)
750ml bone or chicken stock
Freshly chopped coriander

1 If your slow cooker needs to be preheated, turn it on 15 minutes before using. Refer to the manufacturer's instructions for more information on your specific model temperatures.

2 Put all the ingredients in the cooker, apart from the fresh coriander (which you can add later). Make sure the stock is hot when adding it as this will keep the temperature.

3 Cook on low for 6–8 hours, or if you want a faster meal, cook on high for 4 hours. Add half the fresh coriander 20 minutes before the end of the cooking time.

4 To serve, ladle into a bowl, and add a garnish of coriander leaves.

I have shamelessly pinched this recipe from a friend of mine. She first discovered it online and has since adapted it. It is a big hit with her family and friends, so I hope you enjoy it.

Chilli and Prawn Soup

SERVES 4

Nutritional information per serving
232 kcal
14.4g fat
4.7g net carbohydrates
1.5g fibre
20.1g protein

1 bunch of spring onions, finely chopped
2–3 cloves of garlic, crushed
1–2 chillies, finely chopped
2.5cm knuckle of ginger, finely chopped
350g prawns, deveined and shelled
75g creamed coconut
500ml fish stock
4–6 tsp sugar-free fish sauce
Handful of fresh coriander

1 If your slow cooker needs to be preheated, turn it on 15 minutes before using. Refer to the manufacturer's instructions for more information on your specific model temperatures.

2 Put all the ingredients in the cooker, apart from the coriander. Make sure the stock is hot when adding it as this will keep the temperature.

3 Cook on high for 2 hours. Add the coriander and cook for another 20 minutes before serving.

Cauliflower has never been so popular. This soup is one of my favourites, rich and creamy and taking very little effort to make. If I need comfort or want to increase my fat quota for the day, I stir in some grated mature Cheddar or Parmesan cheese 10 minutes before serving, and top the dish with crunchy bacon pieces.

Creamed Cauliflower Soup

SERVES 6

Nutritional information per serving
506 kcal
44g fat
16.8g net carbohydrates
5.9g fibre
7.6g protein

1 onion or leek, finely chopped
2 sticks of celery, finely chopped
2 cloves of garlic, finely chopped
1 large cauliflower (about 800g), cut into small florets
750ml hot vegetable or bone stock
1 bay leaf
1 tsp ground cumin
Salt and pepper to taste
300ml double cream
A handful of parsley leaves

1 Preheat the slow cooker following the manufacturer's recommendations.

2 Place all the ingredients, apart from the double cream, in the cooker and turn to high. Ensure that the cauliflower is covered – if it is not, add some more stock or hot water.

3 Cook on low for 6–7 hours.

4 Add the cream and combine. Use a stick blender and whizz the soup mixture until smooth. Add more stock if you need it.

5 Serve immediately with a garnish of parsley – or chopped, crispy bacon and grated cheese, if you like.

This is a great soup to pick you up when you are feeling below par. I add more chilli and grated ginger when I am suffering from a cold or flu – it works a treat. You can vary the vegetables in this dish, so really it's the perfect soup to use up any surplus vegetables you may have in your fridge.

Feel-good Chicken and Vegetable Soup

SERVES 6

Nutritional information per serving

201 kcal
10.5g fat
6.8g net carbohydrates
2.8g fibre
18.1g protein

1 tsp coconut oil
1 red onion, finely chopped
2 cloves of garlic, chopped
1 chilli, diced
2cm knuckle of ginger, finely diced (optional)
100g diced lardons or pancetta
250g chicken fillet pieces, diced
1 stick of celery, diced
1 red pepper, diced
50g green beans, diced
1 courgette, diced
400g tin of chopped tomatoes
2 tsp paprika
1 tsp thyme
Sea salt and black pepper to taste
750ml hot chicken or bone stock

1 Preheat the slow cooker following the manufacturer's recommendations.

2 I have a multi-cooker with a sauté facility, which is perfect for this soup, but if you don't have this, you will need to sauté the ingredients in a pan. Put the coconut oil, onion, garlic, chilli, ginger, lardons and chicken in the cooker (or pan) and cook until sealed.

3 Place all the remaining ingredients in the slow cooker and turn to high. Cook for 6 hours.

4 Serve topped with grated cheese, if desired.

This soup is delicious and impressive for Halloween. You can use other squashes instead of pumpkin year round. Add some crushed chillies for a little kick if you want to.

Pumpkin Soup

SERVES 6

**Nutritional information
per serving**
102 kcal
1.6g fat
15.4g net carbohydrates
3.3g fibre
5g protein

450g pumpkin, diced
1 red onion, diced
1 clove of garlic, crushed
1 medium-sweet potato (including skin), diced
2 sticks of celery, diced
4 tomatoes, peeled and chopped
2 teaspoons of tomato purée (optional)
2cm grated fresh ginger
1 tsp grated nutmeg
½ tsp ground coriander
750ml vegetable, chicken or bone stock
Juice of half a lemon
Seasoning to taste
Parmesan cheese, shaved, to flavour
Small handful of fresh coriander, chopped

1 Preheat the slow cooker, following the manufacturer's recommendations.

2 Meanwhile prepare the vegetables.

3 Place the vegetables in the slow cooker, then add all the remaining ingredients.

4 Cook on high for 6 hours.

5 Cool slightly. Use an electric hand blender to purée the ingredients, and keep them on warm until ready to serve. Season as required.

6 For an impressive presentation, use hollowed out pumpkins as serving dishes, and sprinkle over the shaved Parmesan and chopped coriander.

4

Low-carb meat dishes

When we opt for a low-carb way of eating, we do tend to eat more meat. There have been lots of conflicting views on the health benefits of meat, particularly in the media. Personally, I feel the benefits of low carb far outweigh any small negatives. I would advise you to always buy the best meat you can afford, if possible opting for organic, grass-fed or free-range products. I prefer to buy from a butcher where I can get information about where the meat has come from, and to know that it has not been altered in a factory. As for any diet, avoid processed foods, particularly processed meats. Many of the recipes below give stock as one of the ingredients – if you want to make your own, there are recipes for stocks in Chapter 9 (see pages 193–4).

This is a family favourite that you can serve on a bed of low-carb cauliflower rice (see page 195), and with some sour cream. You can double up the recipe and freeze any of the dish not used until needed. This version does not include red kidney beans as most people on low-carb diets, particularly LCHF ones, avoid pulses.

Low-Carb Chilli con Carne

SERVES 4

**Nutritional information
per serving**
242 kcal
6g fat
15.7g net carbohydrates
5.4g fibre
27.8g protein

400g sirloin or rump steak, cut into
   chunks, or beef mince
1 onion, finely chopped
1–2 cloves of garlic, crushed
1–2 chopped chillies (amount
   depending on desired flavour)
1 red pepper, chopped
400g tin of chopped tomatoes
2 tbsp tomato purée
250ml bone stock
1 tsp chilli powder
1 tsp ground cumin
3 tsp paprika
1 tsp dried marjoram
80g mushrooms, quartered
1–2 squares of 95 per cent cocoa or
   dark chocolate
Seasoning to taste

1 If your slow cooker needs to be preheated, turn it on 15 minutes before using. Refer to the manufacturer's instructions for more information on your specific model temperatures.

2 If the slow cooker has a sauté option, you can use this; if it doesn't, use your hob. Place the onion, pepper and garlic in the cooker (or pan on the hob) and sauté for a couple of minutes. Add the chopped chillies and cook for a minute more. Add the meat and cook until brown.

3 Place the meat in the slow cooker.

4 Add the warm bone stock, tomatoes, tomato purée, mushrooms, and remaining herbs, spices, and cocoa or dark chocolate.

5 Cook on low for 5–6 hours.

6 Serve with low-carb cauliflower rice and sour cream.

You may not have thought about cooking a moussaka in your slow cooker, but it does work really well for this. Though this is not traditional, I often swap lamb mince for beef mince as my son prefers the flavour. I love to serve this with a crunchy green salad.

Lamb Moussaka

SERVES 4

**Nutritional information
per serving**
419 kcal
30.4g fat
9.8g net carbohydrates
3.7g fibre
24.5g protein

1 red onion, finely chopped
2 cloves of garlic, crushed
400g lamb mince
400g tin of chopped tomatoes
200ml bone stock
1 heaped tbsp tomato purée
2 tsp cinnamon powder
1 tsp dried mint
2 tsp oregano
2–3 aubergines, sliced
300ml crème fresh or cream cheese
2 eggs, beaten
75g mature Cheddar or Parmesan
   cheese, grated
Seasoning

1 Slice the aubergines into thick slices. Place on a tray and sprinkle with salt. Leave to one side.

2 If your slow cooker needs to be preheated, turn it on 15 minutes before using. Refer to the manufacturer's instructions for more information on your specific model temperatures.

3 Meanwhile, in a sauté pan cook onion and garlic in a little olive oil. Add lamb mince and cook until brown.

4 Add tomatoes, tomato purée, herbs and spices, and combine well. Season to taste. Leave to one side.

5 Rub or spray the inside of the stock pot with olive oil to help prevent the moussaka from sticking.

6 Rinse the aubergine gently and pat dry with a kitchen towel.

7 Place a layer of mince in the slow cooker, followed by a layer of aubergine and repeat. Finish with a layer of mince.

8 Cook on low for 4–6 hours, or on high for 3–4 hours.

9 An hour before serving, mix the crème fraîche or cream cheese with the eggs and grated cheese. Season with black pepper and pour over the final layer of mince. Scatter the Parmesan cheese over the top and cook for another hour.

10 If you want a golden top, place under a grill for 5–10 minutes before serving.

11 Serve with a green salad.

A goulash is a chunky Hungarian stew, seasoned with the wonderful flavour of smoky paprika. This is my own low-carb version of this traditional dish.

Beef Goulash

SERVES 4

Nutritional information per serving
344 kcal
10.1g fat
13.3g net carbohydrates
2.7g fibre
46g protein

Olive or coconut oil
1 large red onion, finely sliced
1–2 cloves of garlic, crushed
2 red peppers, finely sliced
500g beef stewing steak, cut into chunks
1 tbsp smoked paprika
400g tin of chopped tomatoes
1–2 teaspoons tomato purée
2 bay leaves
200ml red wine (optional)
300ml bone stock, or 500ml of stock if you are not using wine

1 If your slow cooker needs to be preheated, turn it on 15 minutes before using. Refer to the manufacturer's instructions for more information on your specific model temperatures.

2 Using your slow cooker's sauté facility or a separate sauté pan, heat the oil and cook the onion, garlic and beef until browned, and the onions start to soften. This step helps seal the meat so it's well worth the effort.

3 Return the mixture to the slow cooker if necessary , and add all remaining ingredients. Season to taste.

4 Cook on high for 3–4 hours, or on low for 6 hours.

5 Serve with a few dollops of soured cream.

If you like your food with a bit of a kick, you will love this dish. Adjust the spices to suit your palate. The dish is delicious served with cauliflower rice (see page 195) or – for a winter warmer – some cauliflower mash.

Reggae Beef

SERVES 6

Nutritional information per serving
227 kcal
6.8g fat
9.4g net carbohydrates
3.2g fibre
30.2g protein

500g beef, cut into thick chunks
1–2 tbsp coconut flour
2 tsp smoked paprika
1 large red onion, diced
2–3 cloves of garlic, roughly chopped
2–3cm knuckle of ginger, finely chopped
1–2 chillies, finely chopped
2 large peppers, sliced
2 sticks of celery, diced
2 tomatoes, diced
2 tsp sugar-free curry powder
1 tsp allspice
1 tsp cumin
2 tbsp tomato purée
500ml bone or vegetable stock

1 If your slow cooker needs to be preheated, turn it on 15 minutes before using. Refer to the manufacturer's instructions for more information on your specific model temperatures.

2 Place the coconut flour and paprika in a bowl and mix in the beef, coating it well. Dust off any excess flour.

3 Sautéing the meat before adding it to the slow cooker adds to its colour and flavour. If your slow cooker has a sauté option, this is ideal, but if not heat a little coconut oil in a sauté pan and brown the meat gently for 5 minutes.

4 Place all the ingredients in the slow cooker and set to low. Cook for 8 hours.

5 Serve with low-carb cauliflower rice or cauliflower mash with green vegetables.

I do like food packed full of flavour. This is a very easy recipe that gives you the flavour without too much work. Before I went low carb, this dish had dried apricots and chickpeas in it. To be honest I don't miss them, but if you are making the dish for people who are not low-carb foodies, you may want to add a small handful of them. Check the Harissa paste to ensure that it is sugar free, or use a couple of teaspoons of Harissa powder.

Tunisian Lamb

SERVES 4

Nutritional information per serving
477 kcal
29.7g fat
10.1g net carbohydrates
4g fibre
40g protein

1 tsp coconut oil
500g lamb, diced
1 large onion, diced
1 stick of celery, diced
1 red or yellow pepper
2–3cm knuckle of ginger, roughly chopped
2 cloves of garlic, roughly chopped
2–3 tsp Harissa blend (depending on strength)
1 tsp ground cinnamon
8 olives, halved
500ml bone, lamb or vegetable stock
50g flaked almonds
Fresh coriander leaves to garnish

1 If your slow cooker needs to be preheated, turn it on 15 minutes before using. Refer to the manufacturer's instructions for more information on your specific model temperatures.

2 Place the coconut oil in the sauté pan and add the lamb. Brown the meat, drain it and place it in the slow cooker.

3 Add all the remaining ingredients apart from the flaked almonds.

4 Cook on low for 8–10 hours.

5 Just before serving, stir in the flaked almonds. Finish with a sprinkle of flaked almonds and fresh coriander leaves.

6 Serve with low-carb cauliflower rice (see page 195).

This is a traditional French stew that is normally cooked at various stages over a period of days to make the most of the flavours. You can speed up the marinating process by using a vacuum packer that seals the flavours. This is well worth the preparation for a luxurious stew. Traditionally, this would have been made with white wine – I think red wine goes much better with beef, but the choice is yours.

Daube of Beef

SERVES 6

Nutritional information per serving
241 kcal
9.3g fat
9.9g net carbohydrates
4.1g fibre
21.4g protein

450ml red wine
2 tbsp brandy
3–4 small red onions, quartered
2 cloves of garlic
2 sticks of cinnamon
2 bay leaves
Sprigs of rosemary and thyme
1 orange, quartered, with skin remaining
6–8 sun-dried tomatoes (in oil, drained)
2 tsp paprika
500g stewing beef, diced
Olive oil
1 leek, finely diced
400g tin of chopped tomatoes
150g button mushrooms, whole
50g olives

1 Place the wine, brandy, onions, garlic, herbs, orange, sun-dried tomatoes and paprika in your slow cooker pan and combine well. Add the beef and cover. Leave to marinate overnight in the fridge.

2 Next morning remove the beef from the fridge. Add all the remaining ingredients apart from the olives.

3 Cook on low for 8–10 hours.

4 Half an hour before serving, add the olives.

5 Remove the cinnamon sticks and orange, season and serve.

This is a really simple dish and makes the most tender lamb you can imagine. You can coat the meat with whatever herbs and spices you wish. If the leg of lamb does not fit in your slow cooker, you can either saw off the end of the bone (your butcher can do this), or buy the joint without the bone.

Slow-cooked Leg of Lamb

SERVES 8

Nutritional information per serving
480 kcal
27.3g fat
1.9g net carbohydrates
0.1g fibre
54g protein

Leg of lamb (about 1.5kg)
3–5 cloves of garlic
1 tsp chopped rosemary
Juice of 1 lemon
Salt
Black pepper
400ml bone stock (or red wine if you prefer)

1 Combine the garlic, rosemary, lemon, salt and pepper to form a paste. Rub this into the leg of lamb. Cover and place in the fridge overnight.

2 If your slow cooker needs to be preheated, turn it on 15 minutes before using. Refer to the manufacturer's instructions for more information on your specific model temperatures.

3 Place the lamb in the slow cooker. Pour the bone stock or red wine around the sides of the lamb.

4 Cook on low for 8–10 hours, depending on the size of the lamb joint.

This was one of my dad's favourite dishes. I have adapted it to make it lower in carbs, but it still maintains the flavour. This really benefits from a slow cook – you want the lamb to fall off the bone. Serve with cauliflower mash and steamed green vegetables or ratatouille, keeping back some liquid to drizzle over the plate.

Lamb Shanks

SERVES 4

**Nutritional information
per serving**
446 kcal
23.4g fat
17.4g net carbohydrates
4.1g fibre
37.8g protein

2 red onions
3 cloves of garlic, crushed
2 sticks of celery, finely sliced
1 leek, finely sliced
1 carrot, finely diced
4 lamb shanks
400g tin of chopped tomatoes
200ml red wine
2 tsp tomato purée
3 teaspoons balsamic vinegar
   (optional)
400ml bone, lamb or vegetable stock
1 tsp paprika
2 bay leaves
Sprigs of fresh thyme, rosemary and
   parsley

1 If your slow cooker needs to be preheated, turn it on 15 minutes before using. Refer to the manufacturer's instructions for more information on your specific model temperatures.

2 Prepare all the vegetables, making sure they are roughly the same size so that they cook evenly.

3 Place all the ingredients in the slow cooker. Make sure they are combined well and evenly distributed.

4 Set the slow cooker to low and cook for 8–10 hours, until the lamb is tender.

5 Before serving, if your liquid is too thin stir in 1–2 teaspoons of cornflour (if on a low-carb/grain-free diet, you can use xanthium gum or coconut flour in the same way), dissolved in a little water, and turn up the heat for 5–10 minutes to thicken it.

6 Season to taste before serving.

My mum is a big fan of gammon and likes to cook this on special occasions. I am now converted, too, but I prefer to roast mine for 30 minutes after slow cooking. This recipe is for a Christmas gammon, but if you don't want the spices you can just add the bay leaf and some seasoning.

Slow-cooked Festive Gammon

SERVES 6

Nutritional information per serving
242 kcal
12.6 fat
2.5g net carbohydrates
0.6g fibre
29.4g protein

1kg gammon joint
1 litre of water or vegetable stock
2–3 sticks of cinnamon (optional)
6 cloves (optional)
2 tsp allspice (optional)
2–3cm knuckle of ginger, roughly chopped (optional)
1 orange, quartered (optional)
2 bay leaves
Seasoning to taste

1 Preheat your slow cooker following the manufacturer's recommendations.

2 Place the gammon in the slow cooker.

3 Pour in the water or stock. Add the bay leaves, cloves, allspice, cinnamon, ginger and orange. Season to taste.

4 Cook on low heat for 8 hours.

5 You can roast the gammon after slow cooking it if you want to crispen up the fat on the outside. Remove from the slow cooker, and score with a sharp knife to form diamonds. Place in a preheated oven at 190° C, and cook for 30 minutes until golden.

6 The dish is delicious sliced, and served with parsley sauce and sauté potatoes.

This is a very simple dish that tastes amazing. You can prepare it in advance. If you don't want to use wine, just double up the stock. Serve with seasonal steamed green vegetables.

Pork Tenderloin

SERVES 6

Nutritional information per serving
407 kcal
27.6g fat
3.4g net carbohydrates
0.5g fibre
34.7g protein

1kg pork tenderloin
1 red onion, finely chopped
2–3 cloves of garlic, crushed
2 tsp wholegrain mustard
black pepper
200ml red wine
200ml bone stock

1 Preheat the slow cooker referring to the manufacturer's instructions.

2 Place the pork tenderloin in the slow cooker. Add the onion and garlic.

3 Mix together the wholegrain mustard, plenty of black pepper, wine and stock, and pour onto the tenderloin.

4 Cook on low for 4–5 hours.

5 Drain and slice, ready to serve with green vegetables.

This recipe is based on the traditional Hungarian stew but given my low-carb twist. It is worth searching for a good smoked paprika for the dish – I love the smokiness it adds.

Pork Goulash

SERVES 6

**Nutritional information
per serving**
385 kcal
24.6g fat
9.9g net carbohydrates
3g fibre
27.6g protein

1 tsp coconut oil
1 large red onion, finely sliced
1–2 cloves of garlic, crushed
150g chorizo sausage, diced
500g pork, cut into chunks
2 red peppers, finely sliced
3–4 teaspoons smoked paprika
400g tin of chopped tomatoes
1–2 teaspoons tomato purée
200ml red wine
200ml beef or bone stock
Handful of freshly chopped parsley
150ml crème fraîche (or use cream or
   natural yoghurt; I find that Total
   full-fat Greek yoghurt is the best)

1 Preheat your slow cooker as directed in the manufacturer's instructions.

2 Place the coconut oil in a sauté pan. Heat the oil and cook the onion, garlic, chorizo and pork until browned, and the onion starts to soften. You can omit this step if you don't want to brown the meat.

3 Put these ingredients in the slow cooker, and add all the remaining ingredients apart from the parsley and crème fraîche.

4 Cook on high for 4 hours, or on low for 6 hours.

5 Before serving, add the remaining chopped parsley and stir in the crème fraîche.

The slow-cooked pork in this dish simply melts in the mouth, and the cider and apple work really well with the pork. I tend to use Bramley apples as I like their sharpness, but you can use any apples you like to suit your preference.

Cider and Apple Pork Fillet

SERVES 6

**Nutritional information
per serving**
437 kcal
27.5g fat
9.9g net carbohydrates
0.9g fibre
34.7g protein

1 pork fillet (roughly 1kg)
1 large red onion, diced
2 cloves of garlic, roughly chopped
   (optional)
2 apples, cut into thick wedges
   (not peeled)
250ml stock
200ml cider
A few thyme sprigs

1 Preheat the slow cooker following the manufacturer's guidelines.

2 Place the fillet in the slow cooker. Add the onion, garlic and apples.

3 Heat the stock and mix with the cider.

4 Pour onto the fillet. Add the thyme and season to taste.

5 Cook on low for 5–6 hours.

6 Serve sliced, with cauliflower mash and green vegetables.

This recipe provides a great way to cook pork in advance. It's perfect for dinner parties right through to a simple meal or snack. Make it in in advance and reheat it when you need it. Serve hot or cold.

Pulled Pork

SERVES 8

Nutritional information per serving

279 kcal
10.5g fat
4.7g net carbohydrates
1.7g fibre
40g protein

1.5kg boneless pork shoulder
2 tsp coconut oil
2 red onions, sliced
2–3 cloves of garlic, crushed
2 tbsp sun-dried tomato purée
2 tsp smoked paprika
½ tsp ground cinnamon
½ tsp allspice
½ tsp mustard powder
1–2 tsp erythritol or xylitol
2 tbsp apple cider vinegar
Sea salt and black pepper to taste

1 Preheat your slow cooker following the manufacturer's recommendations.

2 In the meantime, seal the pork. Place the coconut oil in a sauté pan and carefully sear the pork on each side until brown.

3 Place the sliced onions and 250ml of water in the base of the slow cooker.

4 Mix the remaining ingredients in a bowl and coat the pork thoroughly with them, before adding them to the slow cooker.

5 Pop on the lid and cook on low for 8–10 hours, or until very tender and falling apart.

6 Remove from the slow cooker, discarding all the juices and onions.

7 Serve hot or cold with homemade tomato ketchup (see page 202).

I think it is important to keep to traditional family favourites, especially when dieting. Food is not just about taste; it is also about satisfying the mind and not feeling as though you are going without, especially when you eat with your family. This is a favourite in our house. I often double up the recipe and freeze the surplus for later, or use it in a low-carb lasagne.

Courgetti Bolognese

SERVES 6

**Nutritional information
per serving**
291 kcal
19.8g fat
8.1g net carbohydrates
2.7g fibre
18.7g protein

1 tsp coconut oil
2–3 cloves of garlic, finely chopped
1 large red onion, finely chopped
1 red pepper, finely chopped
100g lardons or pancetta (optional)
400g beef mince
300ml beef or bone stock
  (or red wine)
400g tin of chopped tomatoes
2 tsp tomato paste
75g mushrooms, chopped
2 tsp dried oregano
1 tsp paprika
Black pepper to taste

1 Preheat your slow cooker according to the manufacturer's recommendations.

2 If you have a sauté facility in your slow cooker, or are using a multi-cooker, you can fry the bacon and mince in the coconut oil before adding the remaining ingredients. If not, you may prefer to sauté the bacon and mince in a separate pan to brown the mince and crisp up the bacon.

3 Place all the remaining ingredients in your slow cooker. Combine well.

4 Cook on high for 5–6 hours.

5 Serve on a bed of courgette spaghetti.

Note *To make courgette spaghetti, place the spiralised courgette in a sauté pan with a little butter and herbs of your choice (I sometimes add some chilli flakes for an extra kick). Cook for 2–3 minutes until softened but not soggy.*

This dish is perfect for dinner parties as you do all the preparation in advance and enjoy being a host while it cooks, making it all look effortless. It goes well with cauliflower mash and steamed green vegetables.

Boeuf Bourguignon

SERVES 6

**Nutritional information
per serving**
393 kcal
18.2g fat
15.2g net carbohydrates
4.5g fibre
37.3g protein

750g beef steak, diced
1–2 tbsp coconut flour
Olive oil or coconut oil
1 small red onion, diced
1–2 cloves of garlic, roughly chopped
 (optional)
200g shallots
150g pancetta, diced
1 sweet potato, peeled and diced
400g tin of chopped tomatoes
300ml red wine (ideally Burgundy)
2 tsp dried thyme
2 heaped tsp paprika
300ml hot beef or bone stock
150g button mushrooms
Seasoning to taste

1 Preheat your slow cooker according to the manufacturer's recommendations.

2 Cover the beef with coconut flour before adding it to a sauté pan with a little coconut oil. Sauté until browned. Remove from the pan and place in the slow cooker.

3 Add all the remaining ingredients apart from the mushrooms, and combine well in the stock pot.

4 Cook on low for 8–10 hours. Thirty minutes before serving, add the button mushrooms and turn up to high.

5 Serve with cauliflower mash and steamed green leafy vegetables.

I love curries and this is a very simple, 'throw it all in at once' recipe, served with cauliflower rice (see page 195). I am not always keen on cauliflower rice, so often grate or finely chop broccoli and use that instead. I pop the finely chopped broccoli into a microwavable bowl with lid, and cook on high for 4 minutes – perfect broccoli rice with very little effort.

Lamb Rogan Josh

SERVES 6

**Nutritional information
per serving**
560 kcal
37.1g fat
15.3g net carbohydrates
5.1g fibre
39g protein

1kg lamb, diced
2 red onions, sliced
2–3 cloves of garlic, finely chopped
1 green pepper, diced
2cm knuckle of ginger, finely chopped
1 chilli, finely chopped
2 tsp paprika
6 whole cardamoms, crushed
2 cloves of garlic, crushed
1 cinnamon stick
2 tsp ground turmeric
1–2 tbsp sugar-free curry powder
2 bay leaves
2 tbsp tomato purée
400g tin of chopped tomatoes
400g tin of coconut cream
Seasoning to taste

1 Preheat your slow cooker following the manufacturer's recommendations.

2 Place all the ingredients in the slow cooker. Combine well.

3 If more liquid is needed, add 200ml of chicken or bone stock.

4 Cook on low for 8–10 hours for very tender lamb.

5 Serve on a bed of cauliflower or broccoli rice.

This is a really cheap but tasty ham. You should be able to fit 3–4 hocks in your slow cooker, depending on its size. I use water to cook the ham in as I have found that stock creates a very salty ham. One ham hock should feed two people. When slow cooked, the outer skin of the ham does stay white. You can cut off the skin, or if you like it crispy and baked, place the ham in a conventional oven for 30 minutes to finish it off. Flake off the ham and eat hot or cold.

Ham Hock

SERVES 4

**Nutritional information
per serving**
283 kcal
14.3g fat
4.4g net carbohydrates
1.2g fibre
33.6g protein

2 ham hocks
1 red onion, quartered
1 carrot, roughly chopped
2 sticks of celery, roughly chopped

1 Preheat your slow cooker following the manufacturer's guidelines.

2 Place the ham hocks, onion and carrot in the slow cooker. Fill with water until the ham is just covered.

3 Cook on low for 6–8 hours.

4 Remove the ham. Cut away the skin, and slice or flake the ham away from the bone. Serve hot or cold, according to your preference.

5 If you like a baked ham hock, place the ham in an oven preheated to 190º C, and cook for 30 minutes or until golden.

This is a nice creamy dish that is extremely comforting. I serve it on a bed of cauliflower rice (see page 195) or just with some green vegetables.

Beef Stroganoff

SERVES 4

**Nutritional information
per serving**
302 kcal
19.7g fat
5.1g net carbohydrates
1.2g fibre
21.2g protein

500g stewing beef, diced
Coconut oil
1 onion, finely chopped
2–3 cloves of garlic, crushed
300g mushrooms, sliced
2–3 teaspoons paprika
150ml white wine
200ml vegetable or bone stock
Small handful of fresh parsley,
  chopped
2–3 teaspoons Dijon mustard
200ml full-fat crème fraîche

1 Preheat your slow cooker following the manufacturer's recommendations.

2 If the slow cooker has a sauté facility or if you are using a multi-cooker, you can use just the cooker for the next step – otherwise you should use a pan to sauté the beef.

3 Sauté the beef in the coconut oil until the meat has browned. Place in the slow cooker.

4 Add all the remaining ingredients apart from the crème fraîche, and cook on low for 8 hours.

5 Thirty minutes before serving, stir in the crème fraîche to form a creamy sauce.

6 Serve on a bed of cauliflower rice.

This is my take on a wonderful traditional Greek dish that has a lovely flavour. It is best made well in advance as it needs several hours to marinate, then needs to be cooked on the lowest heat for 8–10 hours.

Stifado

SERVES 6

**Nutritional information
per serving**
313 kcal
10.7g fat
10.6g net carbohydrates
3g fibre
40g protein

1kg stewing beef, diced
1 large red onion, thickly diced (or
    about 20 shallots, peeled)
2–3 cloves of garlic, diced
400g chopped tomatoes
2 tbsp tomato purée
2 bay leaves
400ml beef or bone stock
Seasoning to taste

MARINADE
1 tbsp paprika
1 tsp rosemary
2 tsp allspice
2 tsp ground cinnamon
2 tsp oregano
200ml red wine

1 Place the beef and all the marinade ingredients in a bowl. Cover and leave to infuse/marinate overnight.

2 When ready to cook, preheat your slow cooker following the manufacturer's recommendations.

3 Put the beef and marinade in the slow cooker along with all the remaining ingredients.

4 Cook on low for 8–10 hours to make a very tender dish.

5 Serve with some green vegetables.

This is a great recipe to make in advance. I have replaced traditional lasagne sheets with slices of aubergine. I have also made this with sliced courgettes instead of aubergines, and on occasion even with rashers of bacon. All delicious!

Low-Carb Lasagne

SERVES 6

**Nutritional information
per serving**
561 kcal
45g fat
11.5g net carbohydrates
3.4g fibre
25g protein

2 aubergines
1 tsp coconut oil
1 large red onion, finely chopped
2–3 cloves of garlic, finely chopped
1 red pepper, finely chopped
100g lardons or pancetta (optional)
400g beef mince
300ml beef or bone stock, or red wine
400g tin of chopped tomatoes
2–3 tsp tomato paste
75g mushrooms, chopped
2 tsp dried oregano
1 tsp paprika
Black pepper
300ml crème fraîche
100g mature cheese, grated

1 Slice the aubergines finely, lengthways. Place on a plate and sprinkle with sea salt. Leave to rest.

2 Pour the coconut oil into a sauté pan. Fry the onion until soft and translucent.

3 Add the garlic and peppers, and cook for another couple of minutes.

4 Add the lardons and beef mince, and cook until brown. Add the stock and cook for 2 more minutes.

5 Add the chopped tinned tomatoes and stir well, then add the mushrooms and herbs, and season with black pepper. Leave to simmer very gently for 5 minutes.

6 Put the crème fraîche and grated cheese in a bowl and combine. Season to taste.

7 Put a third of this mixture in the base of your slow cooker.

8 Pat the aubergine slices with a kitchen towel, before placing them on the lasagne mixture.

9 Top with a little of the crème fraîche mixture.

10 Continue to layer, finishing with the crème fraîche mixture.

11 Add more grated cheese.

12 Put the lid on the slow cooker and cook on low for 5–6 hours.

13 Put it under a hot grill for a few minutes to brown the top.

14 Serve with a fresh green salad.

Make this recipe well in advance. You can prepare the sauce early, as it take 8–10 hours to cook. Double up the recipe to make extra sauce that you can freeze for other meals. You can also pre-prepare the meatballs and freeze them until needed. If reheating in the slow cooker, ensure all the items are thoroughly defrosted. Place in the slow cooker and cook on high for 2–3 hours.

Meatballs in Tomato Sauce

SERVES 6

**Nutritional information
per serving**
240 kcal
12.6g fat
11.4g net carbohydrates
3.8g fibre
17.7g protein

SAUCE
800g tomatoes, chopped
  (or 2 x 400g tins)
1 large red onion, chopped
2–3 cloves of garlic, roughly chopped
1 red pepper, diced
150ml bone stock (or red wine)
1 tsp paprika
1 tsp dried thyme
2 tsp dried oregano
½ tsp dried basil
1 tsp dried parsley
2 tsp Sukrin Gold
Sprinkle of salt and pepper
1 tbsp balsamic vinegar (optional)

MEATBALLS
400g beef mince
1 red onion, very finely chopped
1 egg, beaten
3 tsp paprika
1 tsp chilli powder (or more if you like
  spicy meatballs)
2 tsp dried parsley
2 tsp oregano

1 If your slow cooker needs to be preheated, turn it on 15 minutes before using. Refer to the manufacturer's instructions for more information on your specific model temperatures.

2 Add all the sauce ingredients to the slow cooker and combine well.

3 Set the temperature to low, and cook for 8–10 hours.

4 When cooled, freeze or store in the fridge in an airtight container for up to 3–4 days.

5 When ready, you can make a start on the meatballs. Simply combine all the meatball ingredients in a bowl and mix thoroughly.

6 Form into small balls and place on a baking sheet. Cover with a sheet of cling film and chill in the fridge for 30 minutes.

7 Alternatively, you can freeze the meatballs at this stage. I normally place the baking sheet in the freezer to firm up the meatballs, before taking them off the tray and placing them in a freezer bag. This way they don't stick together and you can pull out as many meatballs at a time as you need.

8 Preheat your slow cooker according to the manufacturer's recommendations.

9 You can sauté the meatballs in a little coconut oil to help to seal and brown them.

10 Add the sauce to the base of the slow cooker, then drop in the meatballs.

11 Cook on high for 2–3 hours, until bubbling.

12 Serve on a bed of courgette spaghetti (see page 68).

This is delicious served on a bed of courgette spaghetti (see page 68). Lamb benefits from slow cooking, so prepare this dish well in advance and cook on low for 8–10 hours.

Lamb and Aubergine Ragout

SERVES 4

Nutritional information per serving
348 kcal
17g fat
13.8g net carbohydrates
3.7g fibre
33g protein

500g lamb, diced
2–3 cloves of garlic, chopped
1 red onion, diced
1 aubergine, diced (with skin)
400g tin of chopped tomatoes
2 tbsp sugar-free sun-dried tomato
  purée
1 tsp thyme
1 bay leaf
250ml lamb or bone stock
Seasoning to taste

1 Preheat your slow cooker following the manufacturer's recommendations.

2 You can, if you like, seal the meat by frying it in a sauté pan with a little coconut oil. If there is a sauté facility in your slow cooker or multi-cooker, you can do this without having to use another pan.

3 Add all the remaining ingredients and combine well.

4 Cook on low for 8–10 hours, until the lamb is very tender.

5 Serve on a bed of courgette spaghetti.

5

Low-carb chicken dishes

Chicken is affordable and loved by children, which makes it perfect for family meals. People tend to prefer chicken breast to other cuts, but try to experiment with leg and thigh meat as it has a much better flavour, especially when cooked in a slow cooker. You can swap the chicken in any of the recipes for turkey. Poultry is naturally lower in fat than red meat, but still high in protein, which is why it is so popular with dieters. If you are following a LCHF diet, you may want to add more fat during your day to ensure that you maintain a well-balanced intake of high fat, moderate protein and low carbs. Many of the recipes in this chapter give stock as one of the ingredients – if you want to make your own, there are recipes for stocks in Chapter 9 (*see* page 194).

This is an easy recipe, with the chicken cooked in a lovely stock. Serve with seasonal steamed green vegetables or a salad for a light and tasty dinner.

Herby Lemon and Garlic Chicken

SERVES 4

Nutritional information per serving
187 kcal
5.6g fat
3.6g net carbohydrates
0.8g fibre
30.3g protein

1 tsp coconut oil
500g chicken fillets (breast or thighs work well)
1 red onion, diced
2–4 cloves of garlic, roughly chopped
Juice and zest of 1 lemon
300ml chicken stock
1 tsp dried thyme
½ tsp dried marjoram
1 tsp dried parsley
Handful of fresh parsley

1 If your slow cooker needs to be preheated, turn it on 15 minutes before using. Refer to the manufacturer's instructions for more information on your specific model temperatures.

2 Heat the coconut oil in a sauté pan. Add the chicken and cook for 3–5 minutes until it seals and the outer edge turns white.

3 Remove the chicken and place it in the slow cooker.

4 Add all the remaining ingredients, apart from the fresh parsley.

5 Cook on low for 5–6 hours.

6 Just before serving, stir in the fresh parsley.

7 If you want a creamy sauce, you can stir in a few tablespoons of double cream or some crème fraîche.

8 Serve with steamed green vegetables.

This is quite a hot dish, so adjust the spices to suit your own taste. If you double up the recipe, you can freeze what you don't use for another meal. I like to marinate the chicken for at least 2 hours before placing it in the slow cooker. You don't have to do this, but I think it intensifies the flavour.

Chicken Vindaloo

SERVES 4

**Nutritional information
per serving**
260 kcal
12.4g fat
5.7g net carbohydrates
1.9g fibre
30.9g protein

2 tbsp olive oil
1 chilli
2 cloves of garlic
1–2 tbsp vindaloo curry powder
  (sugar free)
1 tsp turmeric
1 tsp ground cumin
2 tomatoes
250ml bone or chicken stock
Small handful of coriander leaves
500g chicken, diced (breast or thigh)
1 large red onion, diced

1 Put all the ingredients apart from the onion and chicken in a food processor and whizz to form a paste.

2 If you want to marinate the chicken, place it in a bowl or freezer bag, pour on the paste and marinate for a few hours. Skip this step if you do not wish to marinate the meat.

3 If your slow cooker needs to be preheated, turn it on 15 minutes before using. Refer to the manufacturer's instructions for more information on your specific model temperatures.

4 Put the chicken, paste and onion in the slow cooker. Combine well.

5 Cook on high for 4–5 hours, or on low for 6 hours.

6 Serve garnished with raw onion and coriander, and with low-carb cauliflower rice (see page 195).

Turn up the heat with this lovely Cajun casserole, perfect for a cold winter's night. I serve it with green vegetables and cauliflower mash – the ultimate low-carb comfort food.

Cajun Chicken Casserole

SERVES 4

Nutritional information per serving

203 kcal
3.2g fat
11.2g net carbohydrates
2.9g fibre
30.8g protein

1 large red onion, diced
2–3 cloves of garlic, crushed
1 chilli, chopped finely
3 tsp Cajun spice mix (see page 213)
2 tsp paprika
Red pepper, sliced
500g chicken pieces (thigh, legs or breast)
2 sticks of celery, diced
400g tin of chopped tomatoes
1 tbsp tomato purée

1 If your slow cooker needs to be preheated, turn it on 15 minutes before using. Refer to the manufacturer's instructions for more information on your specific model temperatures.

2 Add all the ingredients to the cooker. Make sure the stock is hot when adding it as this will keep the temperature.

3 Cook on low for 6–8 hours, or if you want a faster meal, cook on high for 4–5 hours.

4 Serve with green vegetables and cauliflower mash.

Slow-cooked whole chicken is incredibly tender and moist. It sounds obvious, but make sure that the chicken you buy will fit into your slow cooker!

Slow-Cooked Whole Chicken

SERVES 6

Nutritional information per serving
354 kcal
15.7g fat
6g net carbohydrates
2.1g fibre
46g protein

1 whole chicken
Coconut or olive oil
2 red onions, roughly chopped
1 carrot, thickly sliced
1–2 leeks, thickly sliced
2 celery sticks, thickly sliced
150g lardons, roughly chopped
2–3 tsp paprika
2–3 bay leaves
1 tsp dried tarragon
700ml bone or chicken stock
Seasoning to taste

1 If your slow cooker needs to be preheated, turn it on 15 minutes before using. Refer to the manufacturer's instructions for more information on your specific model temperatures.

2 Heat the coconut oil in a large sauté pan. Carefully brown the skin of the chicken in the pan. This will help give it a golden glow without you having to resort to placing it under a grill or in an oven before serving.

3 Place the chicken in the slow cooker. Add all the vegetables and lardons, spreading them evenly around and over the chicken. Scatter the paprika over the chicken.

4 Add the bay leaves, tarragon and seasoning. Heat the stock and pour it over the chicken.

5 Cook on low for 8 hours.

6 You can drain the chicken from the stock, or serve it as it is. If you want to thicken the stock, remove the chicken from it, mix some cornflour with a little cold water (for a grain-free version, mix some xanthium gum or coconut flour into a paste), and add to the stock. Place on high to thicken.

7 Serve with green vegetables.

This is a lovely easy meal to impress friends at a dinner party.
If you don't have port, you can use red or white wine.

Creamy Mushroom and Port Chicken

SERVES 4

**Nutritional information
per serving**
501 kcal
31.7g fat
9.8g net carbohydrates
0.7g fibre
30.4g protein

500g whole chicken legs and thighs
2–3 cloves of garlic, crushed
1 red onion, diced
1 stick of celery, diced
120g mixed wild or chestnut
  mushrooms, halved
200ml port
1 tsp dried tarragon
150ml bone or chicken stock
200ml double cream
2–3 heaped tsp cornflour (or
  xanthium gum for those who
  are grain free)

1 If your slow cooker needs to be preheated, turn it on 15 minutes before using. Refer to the manufacturer's instructions for more information on your specific model temperatures.

2 Put all the ingredients in the cooker, apart from the cream and cornflour. Season to taste. Make sure the stock is hot when adding it, as this will help keep the temperature.

3 Cook on low for 6–8 hours.

4 Half an hour before serving, mix the cornflour with a little water to form a liquid paste, add this to the stock pot along with the cream, and stir well. For a grain-free version, sprinkle ½–1 tsp xanthium gum onto the dish, then stir in well until it is absorbed and the liquid thickens. Turn to high and cook for 30 minutes to help further thicken the liquid.

5 Serve with green vegetables and cauliflower mash.

This is a quick and easy variation of the traditional French favourite. It has a lovely delicate flavour that works well with green vegetables.

Simple Coq au Vin

SERVES 4

**Nutritional information
per serving**
372 kcal
6.3g fat
12.1g net carbohydrates
0.9g fibre
43g protein

500g chicken pieces (thigh gives better flavour than breast)
Coconut oil
200g smoked lardons
12 shallots, whole
3–4 cloves of garlic, thickly sliced
80g button mushrooms, halved or quartered
350ml port or red wine
350ml chicken or bone stock
2 bay leaves
2–3 sprigs of thyme
Seasoning

1 Prepare the vegetables and cut the chicken into large pieces.

2 If your slow cooker needs to be preheated, turn it on 15 minutes before using. Refer to the manufacturer's instructions for more information on your specific model temperatures.

3 Put the coconut oil and chicken in a sauté pan. Add the lardons and cook a little until the ingredients start to brown. Remove from the heat.

4 Add all the ingredients to the stock pot. Make sure that the stock is hot when adding it as this will keep the temperature.

5 Cook on high for 5–6 hours, or low for 8 hours.

6 If the sauce is too thin, mix 1–2 tbsp cornflour with a little water. Add this to the stock pot and turn the setting to high for 30 minutes. If you are grain free you can use xanthium gum – just sprinkle ½–1 tsp onto the sauce and stir well until thickened. Remove the bay leaves before serving.

7 Serve with cauliflower mash and green vegetables.

This recipe is packed with vegetable goodness. It includes curry powder or blends, but do check the brands you opt for as some may contain added sugar.

Nutrient-packed Chicken Curry

SERVES 4

**Nutritional information
per serving**
395 kcal
10.5g fat
16.4g net carbohydrates
5.1g fibre
32g protein

3cm knuckle of fresh ginger, peeled
3–4 cloves of garlic
1–2 chillies, depending on personal
   taste and strength
2 tbsp olive oil
Small handful of coriander leaves
1 heaped tbsp sugar-free, medium
   curry powder
6 tomatoes
1 large red onion, chopped
2 medium peppers, sliced
1 head of cauliflower, cut into small
   florets
400g chicken breasts, diced
80g baby leaf spinach
3 tbsp Greek yoghurt or thick coconut
   cream
Zest of 1 lime

1 In a food processor, whizz together the ginger, garlic, chilli, olive oil, coriander, curry powder and tomatoes until you form a paste. Leave to one side to rest (store in the fridge or freeze until needed).

2 Cut the vegetables to equal size so that they cook evenly. Dice the chicken.

3 If your slow cooker needs to be preheated, turn it on 15 minutes before using. Refer to the manufacturer's instructions for more information on your specific model temperatures.

4 Put all the ingredients apart from the Greek yoghurt and lime in the slow cooker. If the mixture is too thick, add a little water.

5 Turn the slow cooker to auto and cook for 6–8 hours, or if you want a faster meal, cook on high for 3–4 hours.

6 About 20–30 minutes before serving, stir in the Greek yoghurt or coconut cream, and lime zest.

7 Serve on a bed of cauliflower or broccoli rice (see page 195).

I am a big fan of sun-dried tomatoes, and here they are used in a deliciously light casserole. When buying sun-dried tomato paste, ensure that it is sugar free.

Chicken and Sun-dried Tomato Casserole

SERVES 5

Nutritional information per serving
214 kcal
4.6g fat
6.8g net carbohydrates
2.5g fibre
33.4g protein

500g chicken fillets, diced
1 red onion, diced
2 cloves of garlic, crushed
150g lardons or pancetta
1 red pepper, diced
2 sticks of celery, finely diced
400g tin of chopped tomatoes
20g (about 10) sun-dried tomatoes, drained of oil
2 tbsp sugar-free sun-dried tomato paste
150ml red wine
300ml chicken stock
1 tsp oregano
½ tsp thyme
1 tsp paprika
1 bay leaf
Seasoning to taste

1 If your slow cooker needs to be preheated, turn it on 15 minutes before using. Refer to the manufacturer's instructions for more information on your specific model temperatures.

2 You may want to sauté the chicken breast before adding it to the stock pot. This helps to seal the chicken pieces and prevents them from flaking while cooking. If you have a multi-cooker or slow cooker with a sauté facility, you can do this without using a separate pan.

3 Put the chicken in the slow cooker, along with all the remaining ingredients. Make sure the stock is hot when adding it as this will keep the temperature.

4 Cook on low for 6–8 hours.

5 Serve with steamed green vegetables.

I love the flavour of chorizo, and combined with chicken and sun-dried tomatoes it is heaven. I eat this with steamed vegetables (cavolo nero, or black cabbage, is my absolute favourite).

Chorizo Chicken Pot

**Nutritional information
per serving**
286 kcal
12.2g fat
11.5g net carbohydrates
4.2g fibre
30g protein

1 tsp coconut oil
2 red onions, chopped
2–3 cloves of garlic, roughly chopped
2 peppers, sliced
200g chorizo sausages, diced
500g chicken pieces (breast, leg or
   thigh)
2 tbsp paprika
400ml hot chicken stock
400g tin of chopped tomatoes
3 tsp sugar-free sun-dried tomato
   paste, or tomato purée
1 tsp oregano
½ tsp marjoram
Small handful of chopped parsley
30g olives (optional)

1 Preheat your slow cooker following the manufacturer's recommendations.

2 Put the coconut oil in a sauté pan and melt on a medium heat. Add the onions, garlic, peppers and chorizo, and cook for 5 minutes.

3 Add the chicken pieces and brown them before placing them in the slow cooker.

4 Add all the remaining ingredients, and season to taste.

5 Cook on high for 5–6 hours.

6 Serve with steamed green vegetables.

My son loves this and thankfully it is so easy to make. I double up the spices and freeze some paste ready to use whenever we want to add a Thai kick to any meal.

Thai Green Curry

SERVES 6

**Nutritional information
per serving**
615 kcal
47g fat
12.9g net carbohydrates
4.7g fibre
33.6g protein

THAI CURRY PASTE
2–3 cloves of garlic
3 stalks of lemon grass
1–2 chillies, finely chopped (remove
  the seeds if you don't want the
  curry to be too hot)

OTHER INGREDIENTS
1 red onion
3cm piece of fresh ginger
Small handful of fresh coriander
Juice and zest of 1 lime
6 kaffir lime leaves
2cm piece galangal
8 coriander seeds
2–3 tbsp coconut oil
sea salt
black pepper
1 onion, finely chopped
500g chicken breast, diced
1 green pepper, sliced
400ml coconut cream
75g green beans

1 Put the ingredients for the Thai paste in a processor and whizz until a paste is formed.

2 Place the onion and chicken breast in a sauté pan, and cook for 5 minutes to seal the chicken. You can instead sauté these ingredients in your slow cooker or multi-cooker if you have that option.

3 Place the chicken in the slow cooker, then add the paste and all the remaining ingredients. Stir well to ensure the ingredients are evenly distributed.

4 Cook on high for 5–6 hours, or low for 8 hours. If you want to thicken the sauce, sprinkle on 1 tsp of xanthium gum just before serving and stir in well.

5 Serve on a bed of cauliflower or broccoli rice (see page 195).

I love using up my vegetables to make this tempting dish, which is perfect with a bowl of green salad. If you want to increase the fat content, add some crumbled feta cheese before serving.

Mediterranean Chicken

Nutritional information per serving
203 kcal
8.1g fat
8g net carbohydrates
4g fibre
22.2g protein

1 red onion, diced
2 cloves of garlic, crushed
500g chicken thighs
1 red pepper, diced
2 sticks of celery, finely diced
400g tin of chopped tomatoes
20g sun-dried tomatoes, drained of oil
2 tsp sun-dried tomato purée
1 aubergine, diced
1 courgette, diced
50g olives
300ml chicken stock
3 tsp oregano
1 tsp thyme
1 tsp paprika
1 bay leaf
80g mushrooms, sliced
Seasoning to taste
Parmesan cheese, to serve

1 If your slow cooker needs to be preheated, turn it on 15 minutes before using. Refer to the manufacturer's instructions for more information on your specific model temperatures.

2 You may want to sauté the chicken thighs before adding them to the cooker. This helps to seal the chicken to prevent it from flaking into the casserole. If you have a multi-cooker or slow cooker with a sauté facility, you can do this without using a separate pan.

3 Place the chicken in the slow cooker, along with all the remaining ingredients.

4 Make sure the stock is hot when adding it as this will keep the temperature.

5 Cook on low for 6–8 hours. Add the mushrooms and cook for another hour before serving.

6 Serve topped with grated Parmesan cheese.

This has a real kick, but you can cut down on the spices if you want a milder version. You can serve the dish straight from the slow cooker, but if you prefer the more traditional dark and crispy chicken, you can pop it under the grill before serving. Do plan ahead as this recipe needs marinating for a couple of hours before the ingredients are placed in the slow cooker.

Jerk Chicken

SERVES 6

Nutritional information per serving

327 kcal
6.4g fat
5.4g net carbohydrates
2.3g fibre
61g protein

2 cloves of garlic, crushed
2cm knuckle of ginger, crushed
2–3 chillies, finely chopped
2 tbsp dried thyme
2 tsp rosemary
2 tsp allspice
1 tsp nutmeg
2 tsp cinnamon
1 tbsp paprika
½ tsp chilli powder
½ tsp ground ginger
2 tbsp coconut oil
Juice and zest of 1 lime
1.5kg chicken pieces (legs, breast or thigh)
2 red onions, sliced
250ml water
1 lime, cut into wedges, to serve

1 For the jerk chicken seasoning, place all the ingredients apart from the chicken and red onions in a food processor and whizz until smooth.

2 Coat the chicken pieces thoroughly in the seasoning.

3 Place in a freezer bag or covered bowl, and leave to marinate for at least 2 hours (or overnight in the fridge).

4 When ready to cook, preheat your slow cooker following the manufacturer's recommendations.

5 Put the sliced onion and water in the base of the slow cooker.

6 Add the chicken pieces, ensuring that the marinade covers the chicken.

7 Cook on high for 4–5 hours, until the chicken is cooked. Timings depend on the size of the chicken pieces.

8 Remove from the slow cooker. If you want a darker chicken, place under the grill for 5–10 minutes, turning regularly until you have achieved the desired colour and crispness.

9 Serve on a bed of green salad with wedges of lime.

There is something deeply satisfying about using lots of herbs and spices in cooking – and they create wonderful appetising aromas that waft around your home.

Tandoori Chicken

SERVES 6

**Nutritional information
per serving**
342 kcal
20g fat
6.1g net carbohydrates
2g fibre
32.6g protein

1 red onion, finely chopped
2–3 cloves of garlic, crushed
1–2 chillies, finely chopped
1 tsp coriander powder
1 tsp cumin
3–4 tsp sugar-free curry powder
2 tsp turmeric
1 tsp ground cinnamon
2–3 tsp paprika
2cm knuckle of ginger
Grated juice and zest of 1 lemon
Dash of olive oil, or 2 tsp coconut oil
250ml coconut cream
700g chicken pieces (breast, leg or
    thigh)
1 large red onion, sliced

1 In a food processor, mix the herbs and spices with the lemon juice and zest, olive oil and coconut cream.

2 Place the chicken pieces in a freezer bag and pour over the spice mixture. Tie the top of the bag and combine the ingredients thoroughly. For the best flavour, leave to marinate for a few hours.

3 Preheat your slow cooker following the manufacturer's recommendations.

4 Place the onion slices in the base of your slow cooker. Add 200ml of water to the base before adding the marinated chicken.

5 Cook on high for 4 hours or low for 6 hours, or until the chicken is cooked (exact timings depend on the size of the chicken pieces).

6 Serve with a salad or cauliflower rice (see page 195) and a yoghurt dip.

There is a bit of artistic license with this recipe as it would normally have chickpeas and dried apricots in it, but this is a low-carb version. I love using spices to create new dishes – this recipe includes lots of them. Allow the spices to infuse and you'll find that the taste is amazing. If you don't like things too hot you can omit the chilli.

Moroccan-style Chicken Tagine

SERVES 6

**Nutritional information
per serving**
179 kcal
3.5g fat
11.1g net carbohydrates
3.3g fibre
24g protein

500g chicken (thigh, legs or breast), diced
2 tbsp olive oil
2.5cm knuckle of ginger, finely chopped
2 tsp paprika
1 tsp cumin
1 tsp turmeric
1 tsp cinnamon
Small handful of mint leaves
Small handful of coriander leaves
1–2 chillies, finely diced
1 tsp coconut oil (or olive oil)
1 large red onion, sliced
2 cloves of garlic, roughly chopped
1 green pepper, thickly diced
300g butternut squash, cut into chunks (it doesn't need to be peeled)
400g tin of chopped tomatoes
400ml chicken or bone stock

1 Place the diced chicken in a bowl.

2 To make the marinade, put the 2 tbsp olive oil, spices, chilli, half the chopped herbs and tomatoes in a processor. Whizz to combine.

3 Pour the marinade onto the chicken and cover with cling film. Leave to marinate overnight, or for at least 2 hours. When you are ready to cook, bring these ingredients back up to room temperature for at least 1 hour.

4 Preheat the slow cooker following the manufacturer's instructions.

5 If you have a multi-cooker or your slow cooker has a sauté facility, you can use this, but if not, you will need to use a sauté pan.

6 Put a little coconut oil in the sauté pan on a medium heat. Add the onion, garlic and pepper, and cook for 3–5 minutes before adding the chicken, holding back most of the marinade until you add the remaining ingredients.

7 Cook for 5 minutes before adding all the other ingredients, including the marinade.

8 Simmer gently for 5 minutes before adding the remaining herbs, then transfer the ingredients to the slow cooker.

9 Cook on low for 8 hours.

10 Serve with cauliflower rice (see page 195).

6

Low-carb fish dishes

Fish is normally cooked fast and some people may question why you would want to use a slow cooker to prepare it. In fact, you may be surprised at what you can do with it, and at how fish can taste using this cooking method. As a bonus, cooking fish in a slow cooker traps the fish odours so that your kitchen doesn't smell too fishy. Below are some tips for cooking fish in a slow cooker – you may want to adapt your own recipes to suit, or to try something new using this advice. Speak to your fishmonger for advice about the best types of fish to cook in a slow cooker.

General cooking Preparing fish in a slow cooker can really enhance the flavour, but you will have to consider cooking times. We are used to slow cookers generally fitting around our busy lives, but fish recipes may not be as accommodating in this respect as other recipes. Fish does not need to be cooked for long (you are looking at a maximum of 3–4 hours cooking), and it needs to be eaten straight away as it will dry out if left on warm. This may make it less appealing than dishes made with ingredients that can be left to cook all day while you are out at work.

Poaching Poaching fish only takes about forty-five minutes on high. Put your fish in the cooker with stock or water, and simply poach with a few herbs to add flavour.

Shellfish If you like shellfish such as prawns, add them to the slow cooker towards the end of the cooking time, otherwise they may spoil. If cooking on high, this can be done in the last twenty minutes. If you are using frozen prawns, make sure they are completely defrosted before adding them to the stock pot.

My son loves Thai curry and this is one of his favourites. Check the contents of the Thai fish sauce and Thai curry paste, as some brands can contain sugar. If you cannot find a sugar-free paste, you can use my recipe (see page 100).

Thai Salmon Curry

SERVES 4

**Nutritional information
per serving**
396 kcal
26.5g fat
7.6g net carbohydrates
2.5g fibre
30.5g protein

1 red onion, finely chopped
1–2 cloves of garlic, roughly chopped
2cm knuckle of ginger, finely chopped
Juice and zest of half a lime
1 tsp Thai fish sauce
2 tbsp Thai curry paste
400ml coconut milk
500g salmon pieces
200g green beans, cut into
  3–4cm lengths

1 If your slow cooker needs to be preheated, turn it on 15 minutes before using. Refer to the manufacturer's instructions for more information on your specific model temperatures.

2 Put everything apart from the salmon and green beans in the slow cooker.

3 Cook on high for 1 hour.

4 Add the salmon and green beans and cook for another 45 minutes to 1 hour, until the salmon is cooked to your taste.

5 Serve with cauliflower rice (see page 195).

This makes for a light meal that can be served with a selection of salads. You can replace the cod with any other white fish of your choice.

Cod with Pea Purée

**Nutritional information
per serving**
305 kcal
9.2g fat
16.2g net carbohydrates
7.9g fibre
34.9g protein

300g peas
200ml vegetable stock
2 cod fillets (about 150g each)
1 tbsp crème fraîche
Handful of fresh mint leaves

1 If your slow cooker needs to be preheated, turn it on 15 minutes before using. Refer to the manufacturer's instructions for more information on your specific model temperatures.

2 Place the peas and vegetable stock in the base of the slow cooker.

3 Place the cod on top.

4 Cook for 1½–2 hours, until the fish is cooked and flakes easily.

5 Remove the fish and place on a plate with foil covering it to keep it warm.

6 Remove the peas with a slotted spoon – you don't need the stock.

7 Purée the peas with the crème fraîche and mint leaves. Use a processor for this. Season to taste.

8 Pour the purée over the cod when ready to serve.

If you are concerned about using cod, you can opt for a more sustainable fish such as coley or pollock.

Italian Baked Cod

SERVES 4

**Nutritional information
per serving**
202 kcal
7.5g fat
8.5g net carbohydrates
2.4g fibre
24.1g protein

225g cherry or vine tomatoes
1 large red onion, sliced
50g olives, halved or whole
1 courgette, sliced lengthways
2 cloves of garlic
3 sprigs of thyme
4 cod fillets (about 125g each)
2 tbsp sun-dried tomato pesto

1 Preheat your slow cooker following the manufacturer's instructions.

2 Place the tomatoes, onion, olives, courgette, garlic and thyme in the base of the slow cooker. Season well to taste. Add 250ml of water.

3 Spread a thin layer of pesto on the tops of the fillets. Place the fillets on the vegetables.

4 Cook on low for 1½–2 hours, or until the fish is cooked to your taste.

5 Serve with seasonal steamed vegetables or a selection of salads.

Red snapper is packed with protein, selenium, vitamin D and phosphorus. It partners very well with sun-dried tomatoes. If you don't want to use wine, you can opt for fish stock.

Red Snapper and Tomato Bake

SERVES 4

**Nutritional information
per serving**
189 kcal
4.2g fat
8.1g net carbohydrates
2g fibre
26.5g protein

1 tsp coconut oil
2 cloves of garlic, crushed
1 red onion, finely chopped
30g sun-dried tomatoes, chopped
3 ripe vine tomatoes, chopped
200ml red wine or fish stock
Handful of chopped fresh basil
4 red snapper fillets
   (about 125g each)

1 If your slow cooker needs to be preheated, turn it on 15 minutes before using. Refer to the manufacturer's instructions for more information on your specific model temperatures.

2 Put the oil, garlic and red onion in a sauté pan. Fry until the onion starts to become translucent.

3 Add the tomatoes, wine and half the basil to the sauté pan. Cook for another 2–3 minutes.

4 Place half the tomato mixture in the base of the slow cooker. Add the fish.

5 Pour the remaining tomato mixture over the fish, and scatter the remaining basil on top.

6 Bake on a low heat for 1–2 hours, or until the fish is cooked to your taste.

This is a really simple dish – no herbs or thrills, just plain trout cooked in your slow cooker. Putting a few slices of lemon in the base of the slow cooker will impart a subtle lemon flavour to the fish. Exact timings depend on the size of the trout – the cooking time is 45 minutes to 1½ hours.

Slow-cooked Trout

SERVES 2

**Nutritional information
per serving**
344 kcal
14.3g fat
0g net carbohydrates
0g fibre
54g protein

2 rainbow trout, gutted, heads and
   tails removed

1 If your slow cooker needs to be preheated, turn it on 15 minutes before using. Refer to the manufacturer's instructions for more information on your specific model temperatures.

2 Place a trivet, wire rack or upturned saucer in the base of the slow cooker.

3 Add 500ml warm water.

4 Add the trout.

5 Cook on high for 45 minutes to 1½ hours, depending on the size of the trout.

6 Serve with a green salad and vinaigrette dressing.

The vegetables in this recipe add great flavour to the cod. If you prefer not to use cod, you can use any other white fish fillets.

Cod and Vegetable Bake

SERVES 4

**Nutritional information
per serving**
155 kcal
1.6g fat
7.5g net carbohydrates
3.8g fibre
25.4g protein

1 red pepper, seeded and chopped
4 shallots, finely chopped
2 courgettes, diced
2–3 large tomatoes, finely chopped
Handful of fresh tarragon, finely
  chopped
4 large boneless cod fillets (about
  125g each)
300ml fish stock
Seasoning to taste

1 Preheat your slow cooker, following the manufacturer's instructions.

2 Prepare the vegetables, then place them, the seasoning and the herbs in the base of the slow cooker.

3 Place the fish fillets on top.

4 Pour in the stock.

5 Cook on high for 2–3 hours.

6 Serve with a variety of salads or some seasonal steamed vegetables.

Serve this casserole with cauliflower rice (see page 195) and green vegetables.

Halibut, Chilli and Vegetable Casserole

SERVES 6

Nutritional information per serving
197 kcal
4.4g fat
10.7g net carbohydrates
3.7g fibre
21.2g protein

1 red onion, sliced
1–2 peppers, sliced
1–2 chillies, finely sliced (to taste)
1 carrot, diced
2 sticks of celery, diced
400g tin of chopped tomatoes
2 tsp sugar-free sun-dried tomato paste
½ tsp chilli powder
1 tsp paprika
200ml white wine
200ml fish stock
2 courgettes, thickly sliced
500g halibut fillets, diced

1 If your slow cooker needs to be preheated, turn it on 15 minutes before using. Refer to the manufacturer's instructions for more information on your specific model temperatures.

2 Prepare the vegetables, making sure they are cut to equal size and thickness – ideally chunky.

3 Add everything apart from the courgettes and fish to the stock pot. Make sure the fish stock is hot when adding it to the stock pot. Season to taste.

4 Cook for 6–8 hours on low.

5 About 45 minutes to 1 hour before serving, switch the cooker to high and add the courgettes and halibut. Test that the fish is tender and cooked before serving.

6 Serve with cauliflower rice (see page 195).

Fill your stock pot and wait 1–2 hours for a tasty fish pot. You can buy fish-pie mixes, which are ideal for this. They normally include a selection of salmon, haddock, and pollock or cod.

Simple Fish Pot

SERVES 6

**Nutritional information
per serving**
207 kcal
4.3g fat
10.2g net carbohydrates
2.4g fibre
22.6g protein

2 onions, diced
2 cloves of garlic, roughly chopped
4 tomatoes, diced
2 tbsp tomato purée
½ tsp ground cumin
1 tsp paprika
2 bay leaves
1 tsp dried parsley
600g mixed fish (such as haddock, cod or salmon)
300ml white wine
300ml fish stock
Freshly chopped parsley to garnish

1 Preheat the slow cooker following the manufacturer's instructions.

2 Put all the ingredients in the stock pot.

3 Cook on low for 1½–2 hours, or until the fish is done (depending on the size and type of fish you are using).

4 Serve with a freshly chopped parsley garnish.

Fish, tomatoes and olives go so well together. You can opt for any fish pieces or fillets of your choice. I choose a white fish as my son prefers this. If you wish, you can top the dish with some grated Parmesan cheese. I like to serve this with a crisp green salad

Mediterranean Baked Fish

SERVES 5

Nutritional information per serving
303 kcal
10.1g fat
12.5g net carbohydrates
2.6g fibre
19.9g protein

1 large red onion, sliced
2 cloves of garlic, crushed
400g tin of chopped tomatoes
2 tbsp sugar-free sun-dried tomato paste
50g olives (any colour to suit), halved
½ tsp dried basil
2 tsp oregano
Seasoning to taste
300ml white wine
500g fish fillets (cod, pollock, salmon or haddock)
Fresh basil and parsley to garnish (optional)

1 Preheat the slow cooker following the manufacturer's instructions.

2 Combine all the ingredients apart from the fish, and put in the base of the cooker.

3 Place the fish fillets/pieces on the mixture.

4 Cook on high for 1½–2 hours, depending on the size and thickness of the fish.

5 Top with a handful of fresh basil and parsley leaves before serving, if you like.

6 Serve with a crisp green salad.

This is such a simple recipe, but there really is nothing nicer than salmon baked in foil, served with a variety of salads. I prefer to maintain the delicate flavour of the salmon, so this parcel is very basic, just adorned with a little olive oil, seasoning and lemon – but feel free to add anything to suit your own preference and taste.

Salmon Parcels

SERVES 4

**Nutritional information
per serving**
288 kcal
19g fat
1g net carbohydrates
0.4g fibre
28g protein

4 salmon fillets (about 125g each)
1 lemon, sliced
Seasoning to taste
2 tbsp olive oil

1 Preheat your slow cooker following the manufacturer's recommendations.

2 Place 1–4 squares of foil on a worktop (depending on whether you want to cook the fillets all in one or individually).

3 Place a slice of lemon in the centre of each piece of foil. Add the salmon fillet, then top with another slice of lemon.

4 Season thoroughly before adding a small drizzle of olive oil (roughly 1 tsp per fillet).

5 Wrap the foil securely and place in the base of the slow cooker.

6 Pop on the lid and cook on low for 2–3 hours. Timings can depend on the size and thickness of the salmon fillets.

7 Be careful when removing the salmon, as the foil gets very hot.

8 Serve with a salad of your choice.

I love this frittata recipe – I serve it hot or cold, and have even eaten it for breakfast. Just as in the case of any frittata, you can use any vegetables you wish. I normally include whatever needs to be used up in my fridge. This recipe includes fresh salmon, but you can use tinned salmon if preferred.

Salmon and Vegetable Frittata

SERVES 6

Nutritional information per serving
335 kcal
27.3g fat
3.7g net carbohydrates
1.1g fibre
17.9g protein

2 salmon fillets (about 250g), chopped
1 onion, finely chopped
50g green beans or asparagus
60g frozen peas
Zest of half a lemon
6 eggs
200ml double cream
Few sprigs of fresh dill, finely chopped
Pepper to taste

1 If your slow cooker needs to be preheated, turn it on 15 minutes before using. Refer to the manufacturer's instructions for more information on your specific model temperatures.

2 Spray the base of the slow cooker well with olive oil. If you are nervous about food sticking to it, you could line it with baking parchment stuck down with the olive oil spray.

3 Prepare the vegetables and salmon. Layer them in the slow cooker, ensuring that they are evenly combined.

4 Beat together the eggs and cream, and season with dill and pepper. Pour this mixture over the vegetables – it will soak through, ensuring that the whole thing is covered.

5 Cook on high for 1–2 hours.

6 When cooked, remove the pot from the cooker base. Run a sharp knife around the edge to help loosen the frittata. Carefully place a plate over the top of the pot, with the top of the plate facing into the pot, then invert the pot and plate so that the frittata drops out onto the plate.

7 Serve hot or cold with salad.

7

Low-carb vegetarian dishes

Vegetarian food tends to be naturally higher in carbs, so we have to do a little bit of a jiggle when we are putting these recipes together. The key is to avoid too many root vegetables, as these are higher in carbs and starch than other vegetables. If you are on a LCHF diet, you will have to add more natural fats in the form of dairy products, avocados, nuts, seeds and flax oil. Eggs are a brilliant whole food that proves invaluable to low-carb vegetarians.

Forget the calorie-laden kormas – this is a great recipe for vegetarians and meat eaters alike. I like to prepare a selection of curries and serve them together so that the flavours can be mixed up. If you love curries, double up the recipes in this book and freeze any leftovers. You can make up a lovely selection of these dishes and invite friends for a curry night. They will be impressed by all your hard work – though all you will have to do is to reheat the dishes and enjoy the atmosphere.

Vegetable Korma

SERVES 6

Nutritional information per serving

238 kcal
16.6g fat
13.6g net carbohydrates
4.9g fibre
6g protein

2 tbsp melted coconut oil or olive oil
2 cloves of garlic
2–3cm knuckle of ginger, plus extra to garnish
2–3 tomatoes
1 tbsp ground almonds
1–2 tbsp sugar-free korma curry powder
½ tsp cumin
1 tsp turmeric
¼ tsp nutmeg
1 large red onion, diced
1 pepper, diced
1 carrot, diced
½ head of cauliflower (about 150g)
300–450ml vegetable or bone stock
40g green beans, cut into thirds
40g peas
4–5 tbsp coconut cream, crème fraîche or thick Greek yoghurt

1 Whizz the oil, garlic, ginger, tomatoes, ground almonds and spices in a food processor until you have formed a paste.

2 Chop the vegetables so that they are all roughly the same size.

3 If your slow cooker needs to be preheated, turn it on 15 minutes before using. Refer to the manufacturer's instructions for more information on your specific model temperatures.

4 Place the vegetables (but not the green beans or peas) in the slow cooker. Pour on the paste and 300ml stock, and combine well. Add more stock if you need to but remember that it will not evaporate, so if you want a thicker sauce, don't add too much. If you think you have added too much water during cooking, combine some cornflour or xanthium gum (if grain free) with water to form a paste, and mix into the korma.

5 Cook on low for 6–8 hours. An hour before serving, mix in the green beans and peas, and cream or yoghurt. Turn to high and continue to cook for the remaining hour.

6 Serve with cauliflower rice (see page 195).

This is a delicious combination that is easy to prepare. If you want to add more fat to the meal, you can top the peppers with crumbled Feta cheese just before serving.

Brazil Nut and Mushroom Stuffed Peppers

SERVES 4

Nutritional information per serving
523 kcal
43g fat
14.9g net carbohydrates
9.8g fibre
13.2g protein

120g mushrooms (chestnut or a mixture)
1 large red onion
250g Brazil nuts
Coconut or olive oil
1–2 tsp yeast extract (Marmite or similar)
½ tsp dried parsley
4 peppers
300ml hot vegetable stock

1 Put the mushrooms in a food processor, and whizz until they are finely chopped. Do the same for the onion and Brazil nuts.

2 Put a little coconut or olive oil in a pan. Add the mushrooms and onions, and cook until they start to soften. Add the remaining ingredients, apart from the peppers and stock, and cook for 5–10 minutes.

3 If your slow cooker needs to be preheated, turn it on 15 minutes before using. Refer to the manufacturer's instructions for more information on your specific model temperatures.

4 Cut the tops off the peppers and put them to one side (you will need them again once the peppers have been stuffed). Carefully remove the seeds from the peppers.

5 Place some of the mushroom mixture in each pepper. Top with the pepper tops.

6 Place the peppers in the base of the slow cooker. Carefully pour the hot stock into the base (around the peppers not over them).

7 Cook on high for 1½–2 hours, or low for 4 hours.

8 Remove the peppers from the stock and put them under a hot grill to char the skin slightly. Serve with a delicious salad.

This is a wholesome dish that packs a punch. I love spicy food, but you can reduce the chillies if you wish, and remove the seeds if you don't want a really intense heat. Serve with cauliflower rice (see page 195).

Moroccan-inspired Vegetable Tagine

SERVES 4

Nutritional information per serving
106 kcal
1.1g fat
17.3g net carbohydrates
6.2g fibre
3.9g protein

1 red onion, diced
2 cloves of garlic, roughly chopped
1–2 chillies, finely chopped
2cm knuckle of ginger, finely chopped
2 peppers, diced
1 large courgette, diced
1 stick of celery, diced
1 carrot, diced
100g butternut squash, diced
400g tin of chopped tomatoes
1 tsp paprika
1–2 tsp chilli powder
½ tsp chilli flakes (optional)
2 tsp turmeric
1 tsp ground cinnamon
1 tsp dried mint
1 tsp ground mint
400ml vegetable or bone stock
Freshly chopped mint and flaked almonds (to garnish)

1 If your slow cooker needs to be preheated, turn it on 15 minutes before using. Refer to the manufacturer's instructions for more information on your specific model temperatures.

2 Put all the ingredients in the slow cooker. Make sure the stock is hot when adding it as this will keep the temperature.

3 Cook gently on low for 8–10 hours.

4 Serve with cauliflower rice (see page 195), and a garnish of freshly chopped mint and flaked almonds.

Here's my favourite combination – I love goat's cheese! Serve hot or cold with a lovely salad. This dish is also great to have for a filling and protein-rich breakfast, or in a packed lunch.

Goat's Cheese, Spinach and Sun-dried Tomato Frittata

MAKES ABOUT 6 SLICES

Nutritional information per serving
330 kcal
29.1g fat
4g net carbohydrates
0.9g fibre
12.6g protein

1 red onion, finely chopped
20g (about 10) cherry tomatoes
60g spinach leaves
110g goat's cheese, crumbled
6 eggs
200ml double cream
Few sprigs of fresh oregano, finely chopped
Pepper to taste

1 If your slow cooker needs to be preheated, turn it on 15 minutes before using. Refer to the manufacturer's instructions for more information on your specific model temperatures.

2 Spray the base of the slow cooker well with olive oil. If you are nervous about food sticking to it, line it with baking parchment stuck down with the olive oil spray.

3 Prepare the vegetables and cheese. Layer them in the slow cooker, ensuring that they are evenly distributed.

4 Beat together the eggs and cream, and season with the oregano and pepper. Pour this mixture over the vegetables – it will soak through, ensuring that the whole thing is covered.

5 Place on high and cook for 1–2 hours.

6 When cooked, remove the pot from the cooker base. Run a sharp knife around the edge to help loosen the frittata. Carefully place a plate over the top of the pot, with the top of the plate facing into the pot, and invert the pot and plate so that the frittata drops out onto the plate.

7 Serve hot or cold with salad.

This sauce is very simple to prepare and perfect for a busy day. Ensure that you don't cook the spiralised courgettes for too long, though, so you don't end up with a sloppy mess.

Mushroom and Tomato Sauce with Courgette Spaghetti

SERVES 6

Nutritional information per serving
368 kcal
23g fat
13.4g net carbohydrates
4.4g fibre
24g protein

2 red onions, sliced
2–3 cloves of garlic, roughly chopped
80g mushrooms, sliced
6 tomatoes, thickly diced (or 400g tin of chopped tomatoes)
2 tbsp sugar-free sun-dried tomato paste
1 tsp dried oregano
1 tsp dried parsley
½ tsp paprika
2 courgettes, spiralised

1 If your slow cooker needs to be preheated, turn it on 15 minutes before using. Refer to the manufacturer's instructions for more information on your specific model temperatures.

2 Add all the ingredients except the mushrooms and courgettes to the cooker. Cook on high for 3–4 hours. Add the mushrooms 30 minutes before serving.

3 When the sauce has finished cooking, heat a sauté pan with a little coconut oil or butter.

4 Once heated, add the spiralised courgettes and cook for a couple of minutes, until only just softened.

5 Remove the sauce from the slow cooker, place the courgette in bowls and top with the sauce. Serve immediately.

This is a very filling meal – you really don't need to serve it with anything else. Prepare the base in the slow cooker, then add the crumbly topping and pop under the grill. I love the crunchy topping. We normally fight over this in our house.

Vegetable and Chickpea Crumbly

SERVES 4

**Nutritional information
per serving**
371 kcal
26.6g fat
13.5g net carbohydrates
6.9g fibre
15.5g protein

1 red onion, sliced
2 cloves of garlic, crushed
1 leek, sliced
1 large courgette, diced
2 sticks of celery, diced
1 aubergine, thickly diced
½ butternut squash, deseeded and
  thickly diced (skin left on)
400g tin of chopped tomatoes
2 tbsp sugar-free sun-dried tomato
  paste
2 tsp paprika
1 tsp oregano
1 tsp thyme
Handful of freshly chopped parsley
300–400ml vegetable stock

CRUMBLY TOPPING
100g ground almonds
75g seed mix
100g Parmesan or mature Cheddar
  cheese, grated

1 Preheat your slow cooker following the manufacturer's instructions.

2 Put all the ingredients, apart from those for the crumbly topping, in the cooker. Cook on low for 8 hours.

3 When ready to serve, mix together the crumbly topping. Remove the stock pot from the slow cooker. Scatter the crumbly topping over the vegetable mix, and place the pot under the grill until the topping is golden. If you prefer you can spoon the topping ingredients into a more appropriate ovenproof dish, before adding the topping and placing the dish under the grill.

4 Serve immediately with a green salad and cauliflower rice (see page 195).

This is a nice, creamy dish that is extremely comforting. Make sure you combine everything well before cooking. I serve the dish on a bed of cauliflower rice (see page 195), or just with some green vegetables.

Mushroom Stroganoff

SERVES 4

Nutritional information per serving
298 kcal
26.3g fat
8.9g net carbohydrates
3g fibre
5g protein

2 tbsp butter
1 onion, finely chopped
2–3 cloves of garlic, crushed
600g mushrooms, halved
1 tbsp smoked paprika
350–450ml vegetable or bone stock
2 tbsp fresh parsley
2–3 tsp Dijon mustard
Black pepper
300ml sour cream

1 Preheat your slow cooker following the manufacturer's recommendations.

2 Place all the ingredients, apart from the sour cream, in the slow cooker. Season well to taste.

3 Cook on low for 4 hours.

4 Thirty minutes before serving, stir in the sour cream to form a creamy sauce.

5 Serve on a bed of cauliflower rice.

This is my mum's favourite – she eats the slices cold with a salad for a quick and easy lunch. You can use any vegetables for this dish, and it's a good recipe for using up the contents of your vegetable drawer. Lumps of feta cheese can be used in place of the Cheddar cheese.

Crustless Spinach and Courgette Quiche

MAKES 6–8 SLICES

Nutritional information per slice

286 kcal
26.1g fat
1.6g net carbohydrates
1.1g fibre
10.6g protein

1 large courgette, sliced
1 bunch of spring onions, finely chopped
75g baby leaf spinach
120g mature Cheddar cheese, grated
6 eggs, beaten
250ml double cream or full-fat milk
1 tsp oregano
1 tsp parsley
Seasoning to taste

1 Preheat your slow cooker following the manufacturer's recommendations.

2 Ensure that the slow cooker is very well greased. Alternatively, you can line it with baking parchment, which does make it easier to remove the quiche.

3 Place the courgette slices in the base of the slow cooker. Top with the remaining vegetables and cheese.

4 Mix together the eggs and double cream in a jug until combined well. Add the herbs and season well.

5 Pour into the slow cooker until everything is covered.

6 Cook on low for 3–4 hours, until firm to the touch.

7 Eat hot or cold.

This dish is packed with vegetable goodness. The recipe uses curry powder or blends, but do check your preferred spice blends as some may contain added sugar.

Vegetable and Aubergine Curry with Cauliflower Rice

SERVES 4

Nutritional information per serving
395 kcal
10.5g fat
16.4g net carbohydrates
5.1g fibre
32g protein

3cm knuckle of fresh ginger, peeled
3–4 cloves of garlic
1–2 chillies, depending on personal taste and strength
2 tbsp olive oil
Small handful of coriander leaves
1 heaped tbsp sugar-free medium curry powder
6 tomatoes
1 large red onion, chopped
2 medium peppers, diced
1 aubergine, diced
1 courgette, diced
½ butternut squash, diced with skin
3 tbsp Greek yoghurt or thick coconut cream
Zest of a lime

1 In a food processor, combine the ginger, garlic, chilli, olive oil, coriander, curry powder and tomatoes. Whizz until you form a paste. Leave to one side to rest (store in the fridge or freeze until needed).

2 Make sure you cut the vegetables to equal size so that you get an even cook.

3 If your slow cooker needs to be preheated, turn it on 15 minutes before using. Refer to the manufacturer's instructions for more information on your specific model temperatures.

4 Put all the ingredients in the cooker, apart from the Greek yoghurt and lime zest. If the curry is too thick, add a little water.

5 Cook on low for 8 hours, or on high for 4–5 hours if you want a faster meal,

6 About 20–30 minutes before serving, stir in the Greek yoghurt or coconut cream, and the lime zest.

7 Stir and serve on a bed of cauliflower or broccoli rice (see page 195).

Cauliflower and potato is a traditional Indian dish, known as Aloo Gobi. This curry contains a little sweet potato as my nod to the traditional dish. I like to use this as a side dish to other curries, but it can also be eaten on its own. I would serve it with some broccoli rice (see page 195). Note that if you wish to reduce the carbohydrates by 10g, you should omit the sweet potato.

Cauliflower Curry

SERVES 4

**Nutritional information
per serving**
166 kcal
5.4g fat
22.5g net carbohydrates
4.7g fibre
4.6g protein

2 tsp coconut oil
1 red onion, finely chopped
2–3 cloves of garlic, finely chopped
1 chilli, finely chopped
2cm knuckle of fresh ginger, finely
   chopped
1 heaped tsp turmeric
1 tbsp sugar-free curry powder
300g of cauliflower, cut into small
   florets
200g sweet potato, diced
400g tin of chopped tomatoes
300ml vegetable stock

1 Preheat your slow cooker following the manufacturer's recommendations.

2 Place all the ingredients in the slow cooker and cook on low for 7 hours (or until the vegetables are tender). You can sauté the spices with the onion, garlic, chilli and ginger first, which does help to release their flavours. I have tried both ways, and to be honest there is very little difference in the result (except that you save yourself some washing up when cooking all the ingredients together).

3 Serve with broccoli rice.

You don't have to be a vegetarian to enjoy this dish. It is bursting with flavour and so easy to make, using up any leftover vegetables to create a wholesome and nutrient-packed meal. The key here is to try to make the diced vegetables a consistent size.

Vegetable Casserole

SERVES 6

**Nutritional information
per serving**
91 kcal
2.8g fat
10.9g net carbohydrates
4.9g fibre
3g protein

1 red onion, diced
2 cloves of garlic, finely chopped
2 sticks of celery
1 large courgette, diced
2 red peppers, diced
1 carrot, diced
1 aubergine, diced
400g tin of chopped tomatoes
450ml vegetable stock
2 tsp sun-dried tomato purée
1 tsp thyme
2 tsp paprika
1 tsp oregano
Seasoning to taste

1 Preheat the slow cooker following the manufacturer's recommendations.

2 Put all the ingredients in the slow cooker. Ensure they are evenly distributed. Add more liquid if you wish.

3 Cook on low for 8 hours.

4 This is a really filling and wholesome dish, which can be served either on its own or topped with grated Parmesan cheese.

8

Low-carb desserts

We all love great desserts, and a slow cooker can be used to make a variety of delicious desserts and even cakes. Do read the opening advice concerning low-carb flour options and sugar-free recommendations. This is really important to ensure a good bake.

Reduce your sweet palate

I have worked with more than thirty-five schools, where I've reduced the pupils' sugar intake by 40 per cent in cakes and desserts without anyone noticing any changes. You really don't need things to be as sweet as they often are. Start to cut down the amounts of sugar you use gradually – this will allow you and your family to get used to less sweet foods, therefore reducing sweet cravings.

Sweeteners
Refer to Chapter 2 (see pags 10–12) for further information on the sweeteners discussed below.

Xylitol This is a really good sugar alternative that can be used as a direct replacement for sugar, so it's perfect for all your favourite recipes. Remember that it is very toxic to dogs.

Erythritol blends In the UK, I use Sukrin blends or Natvia. Both are available in white sugar and icing sugar forms. Sukrin also does a lovely brown sugar alternative, called Sukrin Gold. Erythritol is not as sweet as xylitol, so producers tend to add a touch of stevia to the blend. Use as a direct replacement for sugar in your favourite recipes.

Stevia This is a very sweet product that does not raise blood sugar and is fructose free. In baking, stevia can be much more problematic than xylitol or erythritol, as you have to be careful how much you use – we are talking tiny amounts since using too much of it produces a lingering aftertaste. I have discovered that stevia drops give less of an aftertaste, but it does depend on the brand. I also think people's sensitivity to the taste varies, so find what works for you. For this reason, all the recipes give the quantities for xylitol and erythritol but not for stevia – the amount of stevia you include in a recipe is very much down to personal taste and the brand of stevia you use.

Flours

Flours are carbohydrates and the aim is to keep the carbs as low as possible. You can slow down the digestion of carbs by opting for wholegrain choices, spelt or buckwheat. If you opt for white flour, this will be digested faster and raise your blood sugar levels. You will also find that you will be perpetuating a sugar craving, even if you use a sugar-free sweetener, which is why it is best to choose a more complex carb flour. In my recipes I recommend wholemeal, spelt or buckwheat flour. You will need to add baking powder in order to make these flours rise.

For a low-carb, grain-free diet, you can swap grain flour for almond flour or another nut flour – hazelnut flour combined with ground almonds works really well in cakes. You can grind nuts to make your own nut flours, which is by far the healthiest option. I use my Nutribullet to do this. Store these flours in the freezer to prevent them from going rancid. I like to use either all almond flour, or a 60/40 combination of almond and hazelnut flours. Some people find that a mixture of coconut flour (see below) and almond flour, with a ratio of three parts almond flour to one part coconut flour, produces the best results.

Coconut flour If you want to use coconut flour instead of grain or nut flours, you need to adjust the liquid in the recipe, as coconut flour absorbs almost ten times its volume of liquid – if you're not careful you could end up with a very, very dry cake! In baking, I've found that the best results are obtained if I use 1 egg and 2 tablespoons of liquid (milk, water, buttermilk or Greek yoghurt) per 30g of coconut flour. Because coconut flour is so absorbent, you need to use less as a substitute for other flours in recipes (roughly half the amount of other flours). It does take some getting used to. *Always* sieve coconut flour before using it because it can really clump up in the packaging.

This takes minutes to prepare and is so lovely when you fancy a dessert. I serve it with a dollop of Greek yoghurt or some thick cream while it is still warm. You can replace the blueberries with any other berries or cherries. Make sure your chosen ramekin dishes fit inside the slow cooker. Alternatively, you can cook a large clafoutis directly in the slow cooker. Grease the slow cooker well with butter, or line it with baking parchment before adding the blueberries and mixture.

Individual Blueberry Clafoutis

SERVES 4

Nutritional information per serving
500 kcal
46g fat
5.9g net carbohydrates
3.2g fibre
13.6g protein

100g fresh blueberries
75g erythritol blend or xylitol (or stevia to your taste)
4 eggs, beaten
Zest of 1 lemon
125ml full-fat milk
200ml double cream
1 tsp sugar-free vanilla essence (optional)
80g almond flour or ground almonds

1 If your slow cooker needs to be preheated, turn it on 15 minutes before using. Refer to the manufacturer's instructions for more information on your specific model temperatures.

2 If cooking the dish directly in the slow cooker, remove the pan from the slow cooker and grease well with butter, then add the blueberries. Combine all the remaining ingredients in a bowl and beat well, then pour over the blueberries.

3 If using individual ramekin dishes, place the blueberries in their bases, then add the combined, well-beaten remaining ingredients. Place the ramekins in the base of the slow cooker. Boil a kettle and pour the hot water around the base of the slow cooker until it is about halfway up the outsides of the ramekin dishes.

4 Cook on high for 1½–2 hours – the top should be a light, spongy egg custard.

5 Serve immediately with cream or sugar-free ice-cream.

I love cheesecake, and this recipe works well made in a slow cooker. You could make a single large cheesecake in the base of the slow cooker, but if you do make sure that you line it with parchment or it may be very difficult to remove once cooked. I prefer to use an ovenproof dish as it makes things much easier. Check that the dish you plan to use will fit in the slow cooker.

Baked Lemon Cheesecake

SERVES 4–6

**Nutritional information
per serving**
461 kcal
43g fat
4g net carbohydrates
2.4g fibre
12.5g protein

6 medium eggs, separated
400g full-fat cream cheese
300ml thick cream
80g xylitol or erythritol blend
 (or stevia to taste)
Zest of 3 lemons
2–3 tbsp sugar-free lemon curd
 (*see* page 198)

1 If your slow cooker needs to be preheated, turn it on 15 minutes before using. Refer to the manufacturer's instructions for more information on your specific model temperatures.

2 Place the eggs in a bowl and whisk until beaten. Add the remaining ingredients and whisk well.

3 Pour this mixture into a greased, round, ovenproof dish. Don't overfill it. You can cover it with foil if you are concerned about liquid from condensation dripping on the cheesecake – this depends on your slow cooker as some produce more condensation than others.

4 Place the dish in the slow cooker. Fill the cooker with hot water to just under halfway up the side of the dish.

5 Cook on high for 2–2½ hours, or on low for 5–6 hours. The cheesecake should feel as though it is setting well.

6 Leave to cool. Place in the fridge to chill before serving.

When I was little, my mum always made me egg custard. I never drank milk so she tried to fill me up with milky puddings. This version still remains a favourite of mine when I am feeling under the weather or need an emotional hug! It's delicious served with a handful of berries.

Baked Egg Custard

SERVES 4

**Nutritional information
per serving**
153 kcal
9.6g fat
5.6g net carbohydrates
0.1g fibre
11.3g protein

4 eggs
500ml full-fat milk
50g xylitol or erythritol blend
   (or stevia to taste)
2 tsp vanilla extract
Grated fresh nutmeg

1 If your slow cooker needs to be preheated, turn it on 15 minutes before using. Refer to the manufacturer's instructions for more information on your specific model temperatures.

2 Beat the eggs well in a bowl. Add all the remaining ingredients apart from the nutmeg, and continue to beat.

3 You can make the custard in a 1 litre ovenproof bowl or individual ramekin dishes. Alternatively, you can pour the mixture into the base of your slow cooker, which should be very well greased. I prefer to use an ovenproof dish or ramekins, as I find it cleaner and easier.

4 Make sure your ovenproof dish fits in the slow cooker, then pour the mixture into the dish. Grate nutmeg over the top.

5 Cover the dish with tin foil and ensure that it is sealed well.

6 Place the dish in the slow cooker. Fill the cooker with warm water to halfway up the sides of the dish.

7 Cook on high for 2–3 hours, until firm.

8 Once cooked, decorate with some berries.

You can use fresh or tinned pears for this, but if you use tinned opt for pears in natural juice and drain the juice.

Pear and Chocolate Upside-down Cake

SERVES 8

**Nutritional information
per serving**
308 kcal
26.2g fat
8.2g net carbohydrates
4.6g fibre
7.2g protein

2–3 pears (drained of any liquid
   if using tinned pears), cut into
   quarters lengthways
100g erythritol blend or xylitol
   (or stevia to taste)
150g butter
3 eggs
100g almond flour or ground almonds
20g coconut flour
40g cocoa or cacao powder
60ml milk

1 If your slow cooker needs to be preheated, turn it on 15 minutes before using. Refer to the manufacturer's instructions for more information on your specific model temperatures.

2 Grease the slow cooker pan thoroughly, or if you prefer, line it with baking parchment.

3 Slice the pears and place them in a nice pattern in the base of the slow cooker.

4 Combine all the remaining ingredients in a mixing bowl. Beat well until you have formed a cake batter.

5 Pour the mixture over the pears and smooth the top.

6 Cook on high for 2–3 hours, or until a knife placed in the centre of the cake comes out clean.

7 Remove the slow-cooker bowl from the slow cooker and allow to cool for 10–15 minutes. If you have lined the slow cooker you can just lift out the cake. If not, you need to carefully place your serving dish upside down (face down) on top of the slow cooker bowl. Using oven gloves, hold both the bowl and the serving dish and flip them over. The cake should drop out onto the serving dish.

8 Serve hot or cold with a dollop of cream or Greek yoghurt.

This is a delicious pudding for when you want a comforting dessert. Use the best-quality dark chocolate you can find, with at least 90 per cent cocoa solids. You can make this in one large pudding basin (I use a 1.2 litre basin), or four 250ml pudding moulds.

Chocolate Steamed Pudding

SERVES 4

**Nutritional information
per serving**
350 kcal
28.8g fat
7.5g net carbohydrates
58g fibre
12g protein

110g almond flour or ground almonds
1 tsp baking powder
40g cocoa or cacao powder
100g erythritol blend or xylitol
1 heaped tsp instant coffee
100ml full-fat milk
1 egg
75g dark chocolate (at least 90 per cent cocoa content)

1 If your slow cooker needs to be preheated, turn it on 15 minutes before using. Refer to the manufacturer's instructions for more information on your specific model temperatures.

2 Place the almond flour, baking powder and cocoa in a bowl. Stir in the sweetener.

3 In a jug, mix the coffee with 30ml of hot water. Stir well until dissolved. Add the milk and egg, and combine well.

4 Pour the mixture into the bowl with the dry ingredients, then beat well with a food mixer.

5 Melt the dark chocolate. You can do this by placing a bowl on top of a saucepan of hot water – don't let the base of the bowl touch the hot water. Alternatively, melt it in a microwave, but be very careful as it can burn very quickly.

6 Pour the melted chocolate into the mixture and combine well.

7 Pour the mixture into the pudding basin (or greased individual moulds), and cover with a round of greased baking parchment.

8 Individual moulds just need to have foil pressed down firmly around the tops.

9 If using a pudding basin, take a square of foil larger than the top of the basin, and make a pleat in the centre to allow for any expansion during cooking. Place the foil over the basin and seal well with string tied around the rim, making sure that it is tight. Make a handle with the string to make it easy to remove the basin from the hot pan in the slow cooker.

10 Place the pudding basin (or moulds) in the slow cooker, and pour in boiling water to three-quarters of the way up the basin.

11 Cook on high for 3 hours if using the pudding basin, and 1½ hours for individual moulds. The sponge should spring back when touched. Be careful not to burn yourself when removing the dish (or dishes) from the slow cooker.

12 Turn the pudding onto a plate and serve with a few fresh raspberries and a dollop of cream or Greek yoghurt.

My son thinks these are great, and a nice way to eat a chocolate cake – a hug in a mug! Dark chocolate chips are used in this recipe, but if you can't find any with at least 90 per cent cocoa content, simply use a good-quality dark chocolate bar and smash with a rolling pin to break it into pieces.

Hot Chocolate Mugs

MAKES 6 MUGS

Nutritional information
per serving
296 kcal
27.4g fat
3.3g net carbohydrates
3.4g fibre
7.2g protein

150g butter
100g xylitol or erythritol blend
3 eggs
90g almond flour or ground almonds
20g coconut flour
1 tsp baking powder
40g cocoa or cacao powder
60ml milk
30g very dark chocolate chips (at least 90 per cent cocoa content)

1 If your slow cooker needs to be preheated, turn it on 15 minutes before using. Refer to the manufacturer's instructions for more information on your specific model temperatures.

2 Make sure your mugs are dishwasher and microwave proof – normally chunky mugs are suitable, but fine bone china definitely isn't!

3 Carefully rub the insides of the mugs with butter to prevent the cakes from sticking.

4 Mix together all the ingredients in a bowl, using a food mixer. Once combined, fill the mugs half-full with the mixture.

5 Turn the slow cooker to high. Carefully place the mugs in the cooker, and fill it with hot water until it comes to just over halfway up the outsides of the mugs. Cook for 1½–2 hours, or until the chocolate cakes have risen and are firm to the touch.

6 Remove the mugs from the slow cooker – use oven gloves for this as they will be very hot.

7 Carefully hold the mugs at the top and run the handles under cold water. This will cool them enough for you to be able to hold them as you eat.

8 Serve hot. You can decorate the cakes with cream or crème fraîche before serving.

This is a lovely sugar-free version of the classic crème brulée, made in individual ramekin dishes. I love this served with raspberries or blueberries. You can also change the recipe to add your own flavours. It is delicious with some grated lemon zest instead of the vanilla extract. Pop a few berries in the bases of the ramekin dishes for another variation.

Sugar-free Vanilla Crème Brulee

SERVES 6

Nutritional information per serving
403 kcal
42g fat
1.2g net carbohydrates
0g fibre
5.9g protein

400ml double cream
1 tsp vanilla extract paste
4 egg yolks
40g erythritol or xylitol blend
4 tsp erythritol (for the topping). I use Sukrin Gold (it looks like brown sugar), but you can use white erythritol.

1 Preheat your slow cooker following the manufacturer's recommendations.

2 Combine the cream, vanilla paste and egg yolks – I use my hand blender or a hand whisk for this.

3 Pour this mixture into individual ramekin dishes.

4 Place the ramekin dishes in the slow cooker. Carefully pour boiling water around the edges of the ramekin dishes until it is about halfway up the sides.

5 Bake for 2–3 hours on low or until the desserts start to set – they won't be totally firm. Remove and leave to cool. I normally leave them in the fridge for at least 1 hour before serving.

6 When ready to serve, sprinkle a little erythritol on top of the ramekins (about 1 tsp on each). Using a kitchen blowtorch, caramelise the tops until golden, being careful not to burn them.

7 Serve with some berries.

This is a really light pudding that is quite addictive. The soufflé-like sponge sits on top of a zingy lemon sauce. Delicious.

Lemon Saucy Pudding

SERVES 4–6

**Nutritional information
per serving**
166 kcal
11.9g fat
3.6g net carbohydrates
3.2g fibre
9.3g protein

100g butter
120g erythritol blend or xylitol
Juice and zest of 3 lemons
4 eggs, separated
1 tsp sugar-free vanilla essence or
  paste
250ml full-fat milk
70g almond flour or ground almonds
20g coconut flour

1 Preheat your slow cooker following the manufacturer's instructions.

2 Beat together the butter and sweetener until creamy.

3 Mix the lemon zest into the mixture.

4 Add the lemon juice, egg yolks and vanilla. Beat well before adding the milk and flour.

5 This mixture will form a quite runny batter. Give it a thorough stir to make sure the mixer has not left anything on the edges.

6 In a clean bowl, beat the egg whites until they form soft peaks.

7 Fold the beaten egg whites gently into the batter.

8 Grease individual ramekin dishes with butter, and pour the mixture into them.

9 Fill the bottom of your slow cooker with hot water up to about 3cm.

10 Add the ramekin dishes, making sure the water comes halfway up their sides.

11 Cook on high for 1 hour, then check. The pudding should have a golden sponge topping that is firm to touch. Depending on your slow cooker, the sponge will take 1–1½ hours to cook.

12 When you serve the pudding, you will notice that the bottom half is a gooey lemon sauce, while the top should be a lovely sponge.

13 Serve with cream or crème fraîche.

I like to serve this dish with vanilla ice-cream or a dollop of crème fraîche. It is quite high in carbohydrates so should be just a very occasional treat.

Poached Pears

SERVES 4–6

**Nutritional information
per serving**
109 kcal
0.3g fat
19.6g net carbohydrates
4.5g fibre
1g protein

350–500ml red wine
120g erythritol or xylitol blend
4–6 ripe pears
2 oranges, thickly sliced, peel retained
2 cinnamon sticks
5 cloves
1 star anise

1 Preheat your slow cooker following the manufacturer's instructions.

2 Place the wine in a saucepan and heat up gently. Add the sweetener and stir until dissolved.

3 Peel the pears, retaining the stalks if possible. Cut the bottom off each pear, so that it stands without falling over.

4 Place the orange slices in the bottom of the slow cooker along with the cinnamon sticks, cloves and star anise.

5 Add the pears – you can sit them upright on top of the orange slices, or lie them down flat to allow more of them to be covered in liquid.

6 Pour the wine over the pears.

7 Cook on high for 3–4 hours, until the pears are soft. Remove the oranges, cinnamon and cloves.

8 Place the pears on a plate and drizzle over with the juice. Serve with vanilla ice-cream, or a dollop of cream, Greek yoghurt or crème fraîche.

This is my version of a low-carb and low-sugar Christmas pudding. I have tried to create an authentic flavour without overloading the pudding too much with natural sugars; it is a good compromise for those who want to enjoy this traditional family favourite. The texture is not the same as that of an all-fruit pudding, but it will certainly satisfy those who are on a sugar-free, low-carb diet.

Low-Carb Christmas Pudding

SERVES 10

Nutritional information per serving
302 kcal
21.4g fat
13.1g net carbohydrates
6.3g fibre
7.4g protein

150g blueberries
2–3 plums, stoned and diced (you don't have to peel them)
75g dried cranberries
1 cooking apple, grated, skin left on
75g mixed nuts (such as almonds, Brazil nuts, walnuts and macadamia nuts), finely chopped
2 tbsp nut butter (can be almond or macadamia)
1 carrot, grated
Grated juice and zest of 1 lemon
4 tbsp brandy
3 eggs, beaten
50g coconut flour
130g almond flour or ground almonds
1 tsp ground nutmeg
3 tsp mixed spice
3 tsp cinnamon
2 tsp allspice
75g suet (use vegetarian suet if preferred)
150g erythritol blend or xylitol (I use Sukrin Gold, a brown sugar alternative)

1 Place the fruits, nuts, nut butter, carrot, and lemon juice and zest in a bowl. Pour over the brandy (you can use more than suggested if you like a rich pudding), and leave for at least 1 hour to infuse.

2 Put the beaten eggs in a bowl. Sift together the flours and spices and add to the bowl. Add the suet and sweetener, and stir well until all the ingredients are well combined.

3 Add the infused brandy mixture and combine with the flour. Stir well and make a Christmas wish!

4 Pour into a greased, 1.2 litre pudding basin and cover with a greased round of baking parchment.

5 Take a square of foil, larger than the top of the basin; make a pleat in the centre to allow for any expansion during cooking. Place the foil over the basin and seal well with string, making sure the covering is tightly fitted. Make a handle with string to make it easy to remove the basin from the hot pan in the slow cooker.

6 Place the pudding basin in the cooker and pour boiling water to three-quarters of the way up the basin. Cook for 8–10 hours on low. The longer the pudding cooks, the darker it will be.

7 To reheat the pudding, put it in the cooker with boiling water, and reheat on high for 2–3 hours.

These individual upside-down puddings look really good and taste divine. If you prefer to make one large dessert, you must choose a dish that is totally sealed (not a springform tin with a loose base), as you will need to place the dish in water. Make sure you grease the dish well – for extra security you could pop a layer of greaseproof paper on the base to prevent the pudding mixture from sticking.

Upside-down Blueberry and Raspberry Pudding

SERVES 4–6

Nutritional information per serving
334 kcal
31.2g fat
3.5g net carbohydrates
4g fibre
7.4g protein

100g butter
100g erythritol blend or xylitol
3 eggs
1 teaspoon vanilla extract
80g almond flour or ground almonds
30g coconut flour
75g blueberries
75g raspberries
50g butter

1 Preheat your slow cooker following the manufacturer's recommendations.

2 Place the butter and sweetener in a mixer and beat until light and fluffy.

3 Gradually add the eggs and vanilla extract. Fold in the flour.

4 Add the blueberries and raspberries. Stir in until evenly combined.

5 Thoroughly grease individual ramekin dishes ready for use. Alternatively, you can use a single large dish or the base of your slow cooker if you prefer. Ensure they are well greased or lined with baking parchment.

6 Pour the cake mix into the ramekin dishes, large dish or slow cooker pan.

7 Place the ramekin dishes or large dish in your slow cooker, and add boiling water until it comes halfway up their sides. If you are cooking directly in the base of the slow cooker, you do not need to follow this step.

8 Cook on high for 2 hours for individual dishes, or 3 hours for a large one, until the sponge is firm to the touch.

9 Remove the dishes from the slow cooker, taking care not to burn yourself as they will be very hot.

10 To serve, carefully loosen the sides of the dishes using a knife. Place a plate over the top of the dishes (with the top side of the plate meeting the tops of the dishes, as you will be turning them

out onto the plate). Hold the plate firmly onto the dish, and flip over. The cake should come away easily and sit on the plate, with the apple and blackberry side up.

11 Serve with a dollop of cream, crème fraîche or ice-cream.

This is a little twist on the traditional upside-down pudding. It works best with pineapple rings, but you can use chunks if you are happy with the pineapple being just in the base rather than all around the edges of the bowl. Remember to grease the pudding basin well.

Pineapple Upside-down Steamed Pudding

SERVES 4–6

**Nutritional information
per serving**
283 kcal
25g fat
5.9g net carbohydrates
3.9g fibre
6.3g protein

110g butter
100g erythritol blend or xylitol
2 eggs
80g almond flour or ground almonds
30g coconut flour
1 tsp vanilla extract or paste
1 small tin of pineapple rings (you
   will need 4–6 rings)

1 In a bowl, beat together the butter and sweetener until light and fluffy.

2 Beat in the eggs, followed by the flours. Stir in the vanilla extract.

3 Grease a 1.2 litre pudding basin well. Place the pineapple rings in the pudding basin – put one at the bottom and place the others around the edge.

4 Place the cake mixture in the basin, covering the pineapple rings. Level the top.

5 Cover with a greased round of baking parchment.

6 Take a square of foil larger than the top of the basin, and make a pleat in the centre to allow for any expansion during cooking. Place the foil over the basin and seal well with string, making sure the covering is tight. Make a handle with string to make it easy to remove the basin from the hot pan in the slow cooker.

7 Place the pudding in the cooker and pour in boiling water to three-quarters of the way up the basin.

8 Cook for 3 hours on high.

9 Turn out upside down onto a large plate. Serve with home-made custard, cream or crème fraîche.

Bakewell tart reminds me of my childhood. It is quite easy to adapt a tart recipe like the one in my *Sugar-Free Family Cookbook* to a low-carb and grain-free version, but this recipe is more of a steamed pudding with the Bakewell tart flavours. It works well with sugar-free custard.

Bakewell Pudding

SERVES 6

Nutritional information per serving
249 kcal
21.1g fat
3.9g net carbohydrates
6.9g fibre
6.9g protein

RASPBERRY JAM
200g raspberries
1–2 tbsp chia seeds

SPONGE
80g butter
70g erythritol blend or xylitol
2 eggs
70g almond flour or ground almonds
1 tsp almond essence
30g coconut flour
1 tsp baking powder

1 Place the raspberries in a saucepan. Heat on a low to medium heat and gently squash to release the juices and break down the berries. After a couple of minutes they should start to look more like a rasberry purée.

2 Once the raspberries have softened and you have more juice, add the chia seeds a little at a time, stirring for a minute or two in between each addition, until a good, jam-like thickness is achieved.

3 Remove from the heat and leave to one side.

4 In a bowl, beat together the butter and sweetener until light and fluffy.

5 Beat in the eggs, followed by the flours. Stir in the almond essence.

6 Grease a 1.2 litre pudding basin or 4–6 pudding moulds well. Put a few spoonfuls of the jam at the base of the basin or moulds. Don't use all the jam, since you need to reserve some for serving.

7 Put the cake mixture in the pudding basin or moulds, covering the jam. Level the top.

8 Take a square of foil larger than the top of the basin and secure over the basin; make a pleat in the centre to allow for any expansion during cooking.

9 Place the pudding basin or moulds in the cooker and pour in boiling water to three-quarters of the way up dishes.

10 Cook for 1½–2 hours on high, until firm to touch.

11 Serve with the remaining jam and some home-made, sugar-free custard.

Full-fat yoghurt is rich and creamy, packed with protein and very good for you. I make this yoghurt using full-fat milk and have even made it with single cream for a really decadent treat. You can buy yoghurt starter kits, but they are expensive and unnecessary – just use some live plain yoghurt to start you off. You don't need to add any sweetener – the yoghurt is thick and deliciously creamy. I serve it with a sprinkle of nuts, berries and flax seeds.

Thick and Creamy Yoghurt

MAKES 1 LITRE OF YOGHURT

Nutritional information per 100g

151 kcal
13.5g fat
4.1g net carbohydrates
0g fibre
3.4g protein

1 litre full-fat milk
250ml double cream
5 tbsp live plain yoghurt

1 Preheat your slow cooker following the manufacturer's recommendations.

2 Pour the milk and cream into the slow cooker, and stir to combine well. Set to high. The milk needs to heat to about 80–85° C, so you will need a thermometer to check this.

3 Once this temperature is reached, turn off the slow cooker but keep the lid on and let it cool until it reaches 40–45° C. This can take another couple of hours.

4 Once the mixture has cooled, remove a ladle-full of milk and mix it with the yoghurt. Pour this very gently around the milk in the slow cooker – do not mix, but ensure it is evenly drizzled over the milk. Pop the lid back on immediately to ensure that the temperature remains constant. It may be an idea to wrap the slow cooker in a thick towel or similar, especially if it is in a draughty kitchen or has an ill-fitting lid. You need to ensure that it stays warm. I have read that some people pop the slow cooker into the oven, wrapped in a towel with just the pilot light on, as this is enough to keep a temperature. Leave overnight (about 10–12 hours).

5 When you have a look at the yoghurt, it may resemble cottage cheese. You will need to drain off the whey. I use a sheet of muslin for this, leaving it to drain naturally for 15–30 minutes before gently squeezing out the excess liquid. This produces a thick yoghurt.

6 Store in the fridge in an airtight container. You can save some of the yoghurt to start another batch.

I love the combination of lemon and blueberries in this dish, which is one of my favourite comforting puddings.

Individual Blueberry and Lemon Puddings

MAKES 6 INDIVIDUAL CAKES

Nutritional information per serving
321 kcal
27.6g fat
4.3g net carbohydrates
5.1g fibre
11g protein

60g butter
100g erythritol blend or xylitol
100g full-fat cream cheese
120g almond flour or ground almonds
30g coconut flour
1 tsp baking powder
Zest of 2–3 lemons
4 eggs
80g blueberries

1 Preheat your slow cooker following the manufacturer's recommendations.

2 Beat together the butter, sweetener and cream cheese until pale and creamy.

3 Add all the remaining ingredients and combine well.

4 Pour into greased individual ramekin dishes. You can scatter some extra blueberries on the tops if you have any left.

5 Place the ramekin dishes in your slow cooker. Pour boiling water around the outsides of the dishes until it comes up to about halfway up the sides.

6 Set the cooker on high and cook for 1–1½ hours, until the puddings are firm to touch.

7 Serve hot or cold with a dollop of creamy yoghurt or crème fraîche.

This is a low-carb, grain-free version of a lemon cake that is super-moist even a few days after it has been made. You can top it with lemon juice, or wait until it has cooled and spread sugar-free lemon curd (see page 198) on top of the cake slices.

Super-moist Lemon Cake

**Nutritional information
per serving**
236 kcal
21g fat
2.3g net carbohydrates
3.7g fibre
8.1g protein

60g butter
100g full-fat cream cheese
100g erythritol blend or xylitol
120g almond flour or ground almonds
30g coconut flour
1 tsp baking power
Zest of 2–3 lemons
4 eggs

1 Preheat your slow cooker following the manufacturer's recommendations.

2 Beat together the butter, cream cheese and sweetener until pale and creamy.

3 Add all the remaining ingredients and combine well, reserving the lemons as you will use the juice later.

4 Line a 1lb round tin and pour the mixture into it.

5 Place the tin in the slow cooker. Pour boiling water into the slow cooker around the outside of the tin until it comes up to about halfway up the sides.

6 Turn the slow cooker on to high and cook for 2–2½ hours, until firm to the touch.

7 If you like a drizzle effect, you can spoon some of the lemon juice left from the lemons over the cake, and leave in the slow cooker for the last 10 minutes.

8 When cooked, remove from the slow cooker.

9 Leave to cool completely – any cake made with almond or coconut flour needs to cool, or it can be very crumbly.

10 Once cooled, store in an airtight container.

These are lovely moist and gooey chocolate brownies. They are super-easy to make, using the all-in-one method in a food mixer. Make sure you line the base of your slow cooker well, as this makes it so much easier to lift the brownies out of it.

Chocolate Brownies

MAKES 8 PORTIONS

**Nutritional information
per serving**
330 kcal
28g fat
6g net carbohydrates
6g fibre
9.9g protein

75g butter, diced
75g erythritol blend or xylitol
4 eggs
40g sugar-free cocoa or cacao
110g extra-dark chocolate (ideally at least 85 per cent), melted, plus extra for decorating
120g almond flour or ground almonds
40g coconut flour
1 tsp baking powder

1 Line your slow cooker, using butter and greaseproof paper.

2 Place all the ingredients in a mixer and combine until well mixed.

3 Pour into the slow cooker, levelling off the top so that the mixture is evenly distributed.

4 Turn to low and cook for 3–4 hours, checking after 3 hours to see if the mixture is cooked and firm to the touch.

5 Carefully take the base from the slow cooker and allow to cool for 10 minutes, before removing the cooked brownie mixture.

6 Cut into portions and drizzle over the remaining melted chocolate. Serve hot or cold. Store in an airtight container once cooled.

If you love chocolate, this is the dessert for you – rich and decadent and very addictive! I prepare the dessert in individual pots and serve them chilled with plenty of cream and berries. A word of warning: the dessert is very rich so you may not want to overload the pots too much. Note that if you can't get a shot of espresso, you can use 2–3 tsp of good-quality instant coffee mixed with 50ml of hot water.

Rich Chocolate Cream Dessert

MAKES 6 PUDDINGS

**Nutritional information
per serving**
420 kcal
41g fat
6g net carbohydrates
2.1g fibre
5.7g protein

300ml double cream
100ml full-fat milk
110g extra-dark chocolate (at least 85 per cent cocoa content), broken
1 tbsp erythritol blend or xylitol (or to taste)
1 shot of espresso
1 egg
3 egg yolks

1 Gently heat the double cream and milk in a pan on a low to medium heat, then add the broken chocolate, sweetener and espresso. Stir well until the chocolate has melted. Remove from the heat and allow to cool for at least 5 minutes.

2 Place the egg and egg yolks in a bowl and whisk together.

3 Add a little of the chocolate mixture to the eggs and whisk, before adding the remaining chocolate mixture.

4 Pour the mixture into greased pudding moulds or ovenproof cups.

5 Place the moulds in your slow cooker and fill it up with boiling water to halfway up the sides of the moulds.

6 Cook on low for 2½–3 hours.

7 Remove from the slow cooker and leave to cool. Pop into the fridge for at least 2–3 hours, or overnight.

8 Serve with some fresh berries and cream, if desired.

9

The low-carb pantry

It is so important to ensure that the foods in your store cupboard
are low carb and sugar free. Jars of pasta sauce can contain up to nine teaspoons
of sugar, and spice blends can also contain unwanted and unnecessary sugar.
You don't have to go without, though – this chapter includes recipes for granola,
lemon curd and even tomato ketchup.

This is a really healthy broth, much better for you than processed stock cubes. It is packed with minerals such as calcium, magnesium and phosphorus, as well as collagen, glucosamine and hyaluronic acid, and a wide range of vitamins. It helps support the digestive tract, boosts the immune system, reduces inflammation, strengthens joints, hair and nails, and promotes healthy skin. Your butcher may be happy to give away bones for you to use.

Bone Stock or Broth

1kg bones (bone marrow, ribs, knuckles and so on)
200ml apple cider vinegar
2 large onions, chopped into quarters
2 cloves of garlic, cut into chunks
2 carrots, cut into chunks
2–3 sticks of celery, cut into chunks
2 tsp mixed herbs
Small handful of parsley (or 2–3 tsp dried parsley)
2–3 bay leaves
2 tsp peppercorns

1 If using meaty bones, place them in the oven and roast for 45 minutes to help release the flavours and nutrients. You can omit this step if you prefer.

2 If your slow cooker needs to be preheated, turn it on 15 minutes before using. Refer to the manufacturer's instructions for information on your specific model temperatures.

3 Place all the ingredients in the slow cooker and cover with water.

4 Cook on low for 24–48 hours.

5 You may occasionally want to remove any scum that forms (it's normal for this to appear on the surface of the water). I use a slatted spoon and just scoop it out.

6 When cooked, remove the stock from the slow cooker and strain. It will form a layer of fat on the top once cooled and settled. Don't discard this – use it as a cooking fat.

7 Place in a jar, freezer bag or silicon ice moulds ready to use in your everyday savoury dishes.

Top tip *I store stock in freezer bags as well as some large silicon ice moulds. The freezer bags can be defrosted quickly by putting the sealed bags in a bowl of water. I pop out a few small 'ice' stocks from silicon moulds to add to dishes such as chilli or spaghetti Bolognese.*

Chicken Stock or Broth

1 chicken carcass
1 large onion, chopped into quarters
1 carrot, cut into chunks
2–3 sticks of celery, cut into chunks
2 tsp thyme
Small handful of parsley (or 2–3 tsp
  dried parsley)
2–3 bay leaves
2 tsp of peppercorns

1 If your slow cooker needs to be preheated, turn it on 15 minutes before using. Refer to the manufacturer's instructions for more information on your specific model temperatures.

2 Place all the ingredients in the slow cooker and cover with water.

3 Place on low for 12–24 hours.

4 When cooked, remove the stock from the slow cooker and strain it, being especially careful to remove the tiny bones.

5 Place in a jar, freezer bag or silicon ice moulds ready to use in your everyday savoury dishes.

This is not a slow-cooker recipe, but I felt it was needed here as I recommend serving many of the dishes in the book with cauliflower or broccoli rice. I cook the cauliflower rice in two ways: in the microwave oven and as a sauté. You can also steam the cauliflower or place whole florets on a baking tray and roast them before zapping them in your food processor – I have never opted for this method as I find the sauté and microwave options really easy. If you prefer the flavour of broccoli, cook it in the same way.

Cauliflower Rice

SERVES 4

Nutritional information per serving
39 kcal
0.4g fat
4.8g net carbohydrates
2g fibre
2.8g protein

1 whole cauliflower

1 Cut off the leaves and stalks of the cauliflower, leaving the florets as you would if you were going to use them as an unpuréed vegetable.

2 Place the florets in a processor and pulse for a few minutes until the cauliflower resembles rice. If you don't have a processor you can grate the cauliflower, but this is messy and more time consuming.

To cook in a microwave oven

1 When ready to cook the cauliflower, place in a lidded container without any water, and pop into a microwave.

2 Cook on full power for 5–8 minutes, depending on your microwave. Stir halfway through cooking to ensure that the cauliflower is evenly cooked.

3 Remove the cauliflower, fluff up with a fork and serve immediately.

To sauté

1 Put a little butter or coconut oil in a pan.

2 Add the cauliflower and toss gently over a medium heat for 5–8 minutes, until heated through and softened.

3 Serve immediately.

Top Tip Whizz up a few cauliflowers at a time and place the uncooked, processed cauliflower rice in freezer bags. You can use this from frozen – just add to a sauté pan and cook through.

Serve this hot as a vegetable side dish (it's perfect at Christmas too), or store in sterilised jars.

Red Cabbage

SERVES 4

**Nutritional information
per 100g**
31.3 kcal
0.3g fat
5.5g net carbohydrates
1.8g fibre
0.8g protein

350g red cabbage, finely shredded
1 large apple, peeled and diced
1 small red onion, finely chopped
1 tsp allspice
150ml red wine vinegar

1 If your slow cooker needs to be preheated, turn it on 15 minutes before using. Refer to the manufacturer's instructions for more information on your specific model temperatures.

2 Place all the ingredients in the slow cooker.

3 Cook on low for 8 hours.

4 Serve hot or cold.

Add a little kick to your cauliflower rice with some Indian spices. If you are using your favourite curry powder, check the ingredients to make sure it doesn't include added sugar.

Curried Cauliflower Rice

SERVES 4

Nutritional information per serving
82 kcal
3.8g fat
6.7g net carbohydrates
2.7g fibre
3.4g protein

1 whole cauliflower
1 tbsp butter or coconut oil
1 small red onion, finely chopped
2 cloves of garlic, crushed
1 chilli, finely chopped
1 tsp turmeric powder
1 tbsp sugar-free curry powder

1 Cut off the leaves and stalks of the cauliflower, leaving the florets as you would if you were going to cook them as whole vegetable.

2 Place the florets in a processor and pulse for a few minutes until the cauliflower resembles rice. If you don't have a processor you can grate the cauliflower, but it is messy and more time consuming to do this.

3 Put the butter or coconut oil in the pan.

4 Add the onion, garlic, chilli and spices, and combine well before adding the cauliflower.

5 Stir gently on a medium heat for 5–8 minutes, until heated through and softened.

6 Serve immediately.

I love lemon curd. I use it to sandwich my lemon sponge together, alongside a layer of buttercream. I also add a dollop to the centre of lemon cupcakes. This is a sugar-free lemon curd, so if you are not used to sugar free, you may want to adjust the sweetener to taste. Similarly, if you have been sugar free for a long time, you may want to reduce the sweetener. I find I need less and less sweetener as my palate has changed so much in the years I have been sugar free.

Sugar-free Lemon Curd

MAKES ABOUT 2 JARS

Nutritional information per 100g
154 kcal
14.8g fat
0.5g net carbohydrates
0.5g fibre
4.4g protein

100g butter
175g erythritol blend or xylitol
Juice and zest of 4 large lemons
(all pips removed)
4 eggs

1 If your slow cooker needs to be preheated, turn it on 15 minutes before using. Refer to the manufacturer's instructions for more information on your specific model temperatures.

2 Put the butter, sweetener, lemon juice and zest in a 1.2 litre pudding basin. Place this in the slow cooker and turn to high. Pour boiling water around the bowl until it comes halfway up the pudding basin.

3 Leave for 20 minutes. Remove from the slow cooker and leave to cool for 5 minutes. Keep the slow cooker on as you will shortly be returning the basin to it.

4 Beat the eggs and pour them, while continuing to beat, though a sieve into the lemon mixture.

5 Take a square of foil larger than the top of the pudding basin. Place this over the basin and seal well with the help of some string, making sure the seal is tight.

6 Return the pudding basin to the slow cooker, keeping the temperature high. Add more boiling water around the basin, ensuring that the water comes up to more than halfway up the bowl.

7 Cook for 1½–2½ hours, stirring a couple of times to avoid any lumps (if you forget to stir and the mixture goes lumpy or curdles, whisk it well with a balloon whisk).

8 The curd should be thick enough to hold when poured from the back of a spoon, but not thick and lumpy.

Variation *For a more grown-up variation, try making a lemon and Limoncello curd. Simply add 30–50ml Limoncello to the mixture. Do this halfway through cooking – any earlier and the mixture might curdle.*

9 Pour the curd into sterilised jars. Cover with a layer of parchment before sealing with the lid.

10 Keep refrigerated once opened.

Get into the Christmas spirit and make this amazing sauce – it will make the whole house smell wonderfully Christmassy.

Slow-cooked Cranberry Sauce

MAKES 1 JAR

Nutritional information per 100g

31 kcal

0.2g fat

5.1g net carbohydrates

3.1g fibre

0.4g protein

500g cranberries

1 cooking apple, diced

250ml water

Zest of 2 oranges

150g erythritol blend or xylitol

2 cinnamon sticks

1 If your slow cooker needs to be preheated, turn it on 15 minutes before using. Refer to the manufacturer's instructions for more information on your specific model temperatures.

2 Place all the ingredients in the slow cooker, and stir until well blended. Turn the cooker to high and cook for 3–4 hours, stirring occasionally.

3 Keep the sauce in a serving dish or jars until ready to use.

This is a lovely ketchup that will keep in airtight, sterilised jars for up to six months. I store mine in the fridge. You can adjust the sweetness to suit your own palate.

Tomato Ketchup

**Nutritional information
per 15g serving**

7.3 kcal
0.3g fat
0.7g net carbohydrates
0.3g fibre
0.2g protein

1 large red onion, peeled and diced
1 stick of celery, trimmed and diced
½ carrot, diced
2 cloves of garlic, peeled and sliced
½ fresh red chilli, deseeded and finely
   chopped (optional)
500g cherry tomatoes, diced
400g tin of chopped tomatoes
8 sun-dried tomatoes, diced
3 tsp tomato purée
2 tsp paprika
½ tsp onion powder
1 tsp garlic powder
½ tsp oregano
1 bay leaf
150ml apple cider vinegar
50–70g Sukrin Gold
Seasoning to taste

1 If your slow cooker needs to be preheated, turn it on 15 minutes before using. Refer to the manufacturer's instructions for more information on your specific model temperatures.

2 Place all the ingredients in the slow cooker. Season to taste.

3 Cook on high for 6–8 hours.

4 Remove the bay leaf. Use a stick blender and whizz until smooth – or use a liquidiser if you prefer. If you like a fine sauce, you can strain the mixture through a sieve before putting it back in your slow cooker.

5 If you find that the mixture is not thick enough, either cook it for longer or add some cornflour (mix 1 tbsp of cornflour with some water to form a paste, before adding this to the mixture). Those on a LCGF diet can use coconut flour or xanthium gum in the same way as the cornflour. Cook for another 30 minutes to 1 hour until the desired thickness is reached.

6 Taste and season again if you need to. If you find that the mixture is too acidic, add a little more sweetener or a few more sun-dried tomatoes.

7 Store in sterilised jars.

This is a real gem and so easy to make. It's perfect for using up overripe tomatoes, or tomatoes on offer in a supermarket. You can make this in a saucepan – if you do, you would use fresh herbs, but the slow cooker is so easy. Feel free to change the herbs to suit your preference. This recipe can be used as a base for a Bolognaise sauce, as a pizza topping or in any Italian-inspired dish. I always seem to have a container of this in my fridge.

All-purpose Tomato Base

MAKES 2 JARS

**Nutritional information
per 100g**

28.7 kcal
0.1g fat
3.7g net carbohydrates
1.2g fibre
0.7g protein

1kg tomatoes, chopped
1 large red onion, chopped
2–3 cloves of garlic, roughly chopped
1 red pepper, diced
150ml red wine or bone stock
1 tsp paprika
1 tsp dried thyme
2 tsp dried oregano
½ tsp dried basil
1 tsp dried parsley
2 tsp Sukrin Gold
Sprinkle of salt and pepper
1 tbsp balsamic vinegar (optional)

1 If your slow cooker needs to be preheated, turn it on 15 minutes before using. Refer to the manufacturer's instructions for more information on your specific model temperatures.

2 Put all the ingredients in the cooker and combine well.

3 Set the temperature to low and cook for 6 hours.

4 When cooled, freeze or store in the fridge in an airtight container for up to 3–4 days.

This is such a versatile sauce, great for adding a little extra to your dishes. I love this just stirred into spiralised courgettes and topped with grated Parmesan cheese. You can also use it as a base for a chilli dish.

Spicy Tomato and Chilli Sauce

MAKES 2 JARS

**Nutritional information
per serving**
28.3g kcal
0.2g fat
3.7g net carbohydrates
1.3g fibre
0.7g protein

1kg tomatoes, chopped
1 large red onion, chopped
2–3 cloves of garlic, roughly chopped
2 chillies, diced
2 red peppers, diced
150ml red wine or bone stock
2 tsp smoked paprika
1 tsp dried thyme
2 tsp dried oregano
½ tsp dried basil
1 tsp dried parsley
2 tsp Sukrin Gold
Sprinkle of salt and pepper

1 If your slow cooker needs to be preheated, turn it on 15 minutes before using. Refer to the manufacturer's instructions for more information on your specific model temperatures.

2 Put all the ingredients in the cooker and combine well.

3 Set the temperature to low and cook for 6 hours.

4 When cooled, freeze or store in the fridge in an airtight container for up to 3–4 days.

Make sugar-free and grain-free granola in a conventional oven (baked at 180° C for 8–10 minutes), or use your slow cooker. I find the slow cooker is far more forgiving! This recipe is one for the kids. It is really easy to make and there is nothing stopping you doubling or tripling the recipe to make up a large batch, as it keeps well in a sealed, airtight container.

Choco Nutty Granola

MAKES ABOUT 20 SERVINGS

Nutritional information per 30g serving

187 kcal

17.1g fat

2.4g net carbohydrates

2.5g fibre

4.3g protein

300g mixed nuts (Brazil nuts, hazelnuts, almonds, macadamia nuts, walnuts)

100g pecan nuts (these add a sweetness that kids love)

75g flaked almonds

100g coconut flakes

75g sunflower seeds

75g pumpkin seeds

50g coconut oil, melted

2 tbsp cocoa or cacao powder

2 tbsp erythritol blend or xylitol (or to taste)

1 Preheat your slow cooker following the manufacturer's recommendations.

2 Place the whole nuts in a freezer bag and bash with a rolling pin until they are in smaller, bite-size pieces. I like doing this by hand as it takes out my frustrations, but I also find that a processor tends to over process the nuts, so that if you are not careful you can end up with nutty dust!

3 Place the crushed nuts in a bowl and add the pecan nuts, flaked almonds, coconut flakes and seeds.

4 Melt the coconut oil in a jug placed in a microwave oven for 10 seconds (alternatively, melt it in a bowl set over hot water). Add the cocoa and sweetener, and combine well.

5 Pour this over the nut/seed mix and stir well until the oil coats all the nuts.

6 Pour into the slow cooker, and cook on high for 1½–2 hours, stirring occasionally.

7 Remove from the slow cooker and allow to cool before storing in an airtight container.

This is a more grown-up granola than the one in the previous recipe. I love eating it with natural Greek yoghurt. You could add some fruits to the granola after it has been cooked, but this will increase your carbohydrate and fructose load so be very careful, especially with dried fruits.

Cinnamon Nut Granola

MAKES ABOUT 20 SERVINGS

**Nutritional information
per 30g serving**
189 kcal
17.2g fat
2.3g net carbohydrates
2.9g fibre
4.4g protein

300g mixed nuts (Brazil nuts, hazelnuts, almonds, macadamia nuts, walnuts)
100g pecan nuts
60g flaked almonds
100g coconut flakes
75g sunflower seeds
75g pumpkin seeds
50g flaxseeds
50g coconut oil, melted
2 tsp cinnamon
2 tbsp xylitol or erythritol blend (or to taste)

1 Preheat your slow cooker following the manufacturer's recommendations.

2 Place the whole nuts in a freezer bag and bash them with a rolling pin until they are in smaller bite-size pieces.

3 Place the crushed nuts in a bowl and add the pecan nuts, flaked almonds, coconut flakes and seeds.

4 Melt the coconut oil in a jug placed in a microwave oven for 10 seconds (alternatively, melt it in a bowl set over hot water). Add the cinnamon and sweetener, and combine well.

5 Add to the nut and seed mix and stir well, until the oil coats all the nuts.

6 Pour the mixture into the slow cooker. Cook on high for 1½–2 hours, stirring occasionally.

7 Remove from the slow cooker and allow to cool before storing in an airtight container.

It is a sad fact that most of the spice blends in our supermarkets contain added sugar. This is frustrating as we really don't need it, and it's time the food manufacturers recognised that fact. In the meantime, do as I do and make up your own spice mixes. I store them in small jars until needed. All the recipes below can be doubled or even tripled if you want to store the blends in larger quantities. It is most economical if you buy your basic herbs in bulk.

Spice Blends

Southern Chicken Spice Mix

This can be used on any chicken dish, or as a coating for KFC-style or chicken nuggets. Combine the ingredients well before placing the blend in a jar until needed.

MAKES ABOUT 200G

150g ground almonds or
   coconut flour
4 tsp paprika
2 tsp parsley
3 tsp sugar-free chicken bouillon
2 tsp oregano
1tsp tarragon
2 tsp thyme
2 tsp garlic powder
1 tsp onion salt
1 tsp celery salt
Generous seasoning of black pepper
   and sea salt

Seasoning Blends

For each of the recipes below, place all the ingredients in a bowl, and combine well before storing in an airtight jar.

EACH BLEND MAKES
20–30G SEASONING

Fajita Seasoning

4 tsp chilli powder
4 tsp garlic powder
6 tsp paprika
4 tsp oregano
2 tsp cumin
4 tsp onion powder
2 tsp parsley

Cajun Spice Mix

2 tsp garlic powder
3 tsp paprika
1 tsp onion powder
1 tsp cayenne pepper
2 tsp oregano
1 tsp chilli powder
½ tsp salt
½ tsp black pepper

Curry Blend

6 tsp ground coriander
3 tsp cumin
4 tsp turmeric
1 tsp ground mustard seeds
½ tsp ground ginger
1 tsp chilli powder (add more
   if you like it very hot)
½ tsp garlic powder
½ tsp onion powder
½ tsp ground nutmeg
½ tsp cayenne pepper

Moroccan Seasoning

3 tsp paprika
1 tsp ground cinnamon
½ tsp garlic powder
½ tsp onion powder
1 tsp cumin
2 tsp ground coriander
½ tsp cayenne pepper
½ tsp allspice

Italian Seasoning

4 tsp oregano
2 tsp thyme
1 tsp basil
4 tsp parsley
1 tsp garlic powder
½ tsp onion powder

Index